Borgo Cataloging Guides
Number One
ISSN 0891-9615

A GUIDE TO
SCIENCE FICTION AND FANTASY
in the Library of Congress
Classification Scheme

*Second Edition,
Revised and Expanded*

Michael Burgess
California State University, San Bernardino

R. REGINALD
The Borgo Press
San Bernardino, California □ MCMLXXXVIII

For *Buckley Barrett*, *Cataloger*, and for
Margaret, Denise, Maisie, Cheryl, Lee, Beverly,
Tony, Kris, Carol, and Johnnie, for laughing
at my jokes, and for being such good company

CONTENTS

Introduction		3
I.	Subject Headings	5
II.	Classification Numbers	27
	Index to Classification Numbers	49
III.	Author Main Entries and Literature Numbers	58
	LC Literature Tables	155
IV.	Artist Main Entries and Artist Numbers	159
V.	Motion Picture Main Entries and Numbers	162
VI.	Television & Radio Program Main Entries and Numbers	165
VII.	Comic Strip Main Entries and Numbers	167

Library of Congress Cataloging-in-Publication Data:

Burgess, Michael, 1948-
   A guide to science fiction and fantasy in the Library of Congress classification scheme.

  (Borgo cataloging guides, ISSN 0891-9615 ; no. 1)
  Includes index.
    1. Classification—Books—Science fiction. 2. Classification—Books—Fantastic literature. 3. Classification, Library of Congress. 4. Science fiction—Bibliography—Methodology. 5. Fantastic literature—Bibliography—Methodology. I. Title. II. Series.
Z697.F29B87 1988   025.4'6813'0876   87-6308
ISBN 0-89370-827-5 (cloth, $22.95)
ISBN 0-89370-927-1 (paper, $12.95)

Copyright © 1984, 1988 by Michael Burgess.
All rights reserved. No part of this book may be reproduced in any form without the expressed written consent of the author. Printed in the United States of America by Van Volumes Ltd., Wilbraham, MA.

Produced, designed, and published by R. Reginald, The Borgo Press, P.O. Box 2845, San Bernardino, CA 92406, USA. Cover design by Highpoint Type & Graphics, Pomona, CA.

Second Edition——February, 1988

INTRODUCTION

This second edition of my first cataloging manual has been extensively revised and expanded from the first, having been prepared in tandem with similar manuals on mystery and western fiction. The revisions are due both to my own increased experience and knowledge of cataloging, access to additional reference tools (particularly the Library of Congress's Name-Authority File), a visit to LC itself in 1986, and the continuing expansion of science fiction and fantasy literature. As before, this book is a guide to the cataloging of fantastic literature (*i.e.*, science fiction, fantasy, and supernatural horror fiction, with peripheral coverage of utopian, gothic, and macabre literature) in the Library of Congress classification scheme, including the primary subject headings, classification numbers, author main entries and literature numbers, and the main entries and class numbers of artists, motion pictures, TV programs, and comics associated with the field.

The list of authors has been derived in large part from my books, *Science Fiction and Fantasy Literature, a Checklist, 1700-1974* (Gale Research Co., 1979), and *Science Fiction and Fantasy Literature, a Supplement, 1975-1986* (Gale Research Co., 1988). As with the first edition of this book, I have concentrated on those authors apt to be found in the modern collection of fantastic literature, most of them active in the post-World War II era; fewer writers of horror fiction are included than those working exclusively in SF or fantasy. Also listed are mainstream authors who have written one or two books in the genre. Those authors not included are generally obscure even within the field; most also lack literature numbers.

I presume here some general familiarity on the reader's part with cataloging theory and practice, and with the LC classification scheme in particular, although I have made an effort to explain general principles and specific applications more fully for the neophyte or fan. The science of cataloging may be compared to the practice of law, in that it uses a set of logical rules, plus a series of precedents interpreting those rules, to determine how specific books may be classed. As with the law, cataloging has many quirks, inconsistencies, and exceptions, and may be applied differently by different practitioners; nonetheless, behind these rules and practices there is an established, logical body of thought that is intended to work in a certain fashion and to do certain things. I have tried to provide here some basis for understanding how LC classifies literature, so that even the beginner may gain some insight into what those little numbers on the spine of a book actually mean.

The release in 1978 of the Second Edition of the *Anglo-American Cataloging Rules* (popularly known as AACR2) caused an uproar among librarians, who immediately began taking sides over the question of whether the massive changes proposed in the rules should be adopted. This question was largely settled when the Library of Congress agreed to accept AACR2 in 1980, since LC generates the cataloging records which most large American libraries (particularly in academe) follow. It was only later that the library world discovered, much to its collective dismay, that LC's adoption of AACR2 was somewhat conditional, in that, under long-established LC policy, books were not recataloged retroactively, and main entries which should have been changed under AACR2 were not—and have not—been altered (as they should have been). Thus, while the rules themselves are fairly explicit, their interpretation remains in many cases obscure; furthermore, the nature of both cataloging and literature is such that many of the proposed changes have yet to be applied by LC to specific authors—*and may never be!* In addition, the practices of individual catalogers, even at LC, vary slightly; such variations have increased under the pressure of AACR2. Finally, the influence of OCLC (On-Line Computer Library Center, Inc.), the largest cataloging service and database in North America (with some 7500 member libraries and 17,000,000+ bibliographical records in 1987), continues to grow, and is beginning to serve as a counterbalance to both AACR2 and LC; where OCLC practice differs from AACR2, I have always accepted the former.

    I could not have completed this book without the cooperation of two former Tech Services librarians, Arthur E. Nelson, now Library Director at California State University, San Bernardino, and Marty Bloomberg, Associate Library Director, who supported my requests for release time, graciously allowed me the use of the facilities, and were always interested in "talking shop." To both of these gentlemen, my heartfelt thanks. My appreciation also to Johnnie Ann Ralph, former Head of Material Services at CSUSB. Whatever cataloging wisdom I've acquired I owe to my instructor at USC, Vivian Prince, and to Mike Brown, Head of Technical Services at Cal State when I joined the staff there in 1970. I also wish to thank my friend and colleague at Cal State, Buckley Barrett, currently Head of Material Services, and a Class-A cataloger in his own right, who was with me when we copped the ten millionth record in OCLC. Finally, a tip of the hat to my long-suffering wife, Mary, who has allowed me to continue working on these manuals—when I should have been doing something else!

Michael Burgess,
Chief Cataloger,
Pfau Library,
California State University,
San Bernardino

I
SUBJECT HEADINGS

INTRODUCTION

This section includes Library of Congress subject headings in use through mid-1987, plus any major headings which have been cancelled as of that date (so indicated below). Also listed are the standard subdivisions which have actually been used by LC; these may seem repetitious to the casual observer, but I have included them anyway to provide the researcher with some indication where the major scholarly activity in the field is taking place.

Most of the entries require little explanation. Anthologies of stories by more than one author are usually classed under the main subject of the anthology (*e.g.*, "Science fiction") without further subdivision. Such headings may also be applied to nonfiction books. Books about fictitious characters customarily receive two headings: the first includes the name of the character plus description appellation [*e.g.*, "Tarzan (Fictitious character)"]; the second reflects the name of the writer (*e.g.*, "Burroughs, Edgar Rice, 1875-1950—Characters—Tarzan"). Such books are classed under the author's literature number as criticism.

Books about the work of a specific writer use the main entry of the writer as established under AACR2, plus the standard subdivision, "Criticism and interpretation." A biography or autobiography generally has as its subject the name of the author, without further subdivision. There are, of course, many other standard subdivisions which may be applied to authors, some of which may be found at the end of this section.

I have used pre-AACR2 filing rules here only because the breakdowns of subdivisions are easier to follow with this arrangement. Completists should note that current rules actually require filing these headings on a strict, word-by-word basis, thus intermingling national subheadings (*e.g.*, "Science fiction, American") with the subdivisions under the heading, "Science fiction."

It is also worth noting that the number of subject headings in the SF field (undoubtedly reflecting fan interest) vastly exceeds those in my other two manuals, and that the number of corresponding classification numbers is similarly large compared to the mystery and western genres.

SCIENCE FICTION SUBJECT HEADINGS

Analog science fact & science fiction—Indexes.
Androids—Fiction.
Animation (Cinematography)
Atomic warfare... [cancelled; see: Nuclear warfare...]
Atomic warfare and literature. [cancelled]
Atomic warfare in moving-pictures. [cancelled]
Automata—Fiction. [cancelled; see: Robots—Fiction]
Automata in literature. [cancelled; see: Robots in literature]
Bibliography—Bibliography—Fantastic fiction.
Bibliography—Bibliography—Science fiction.
Burroughs, Edgar Rice, 1875-1950—Characters—Tarzan.
Cataloging of fantastic literature.
Cataloging of science fiction.
Cinematography—Special effects.
Civilization, Subterranean.
Classification—Books—Fantastic literature.
Classification—Books—Science fiction.
Cosmogony—Literary collections.
Creation—Literary collections.
Dorsai (Imaginary place)
Dracula, Count (Fictitious character)
    "   —Juvenile literature.
    "   —Name.
    "   —Poetry.
Dragons—Fiction.
Dragons—Juvenile fiction.
Dragons in art.
    "   Exhibitions.
Dragons in literature.
    "   —Handbooks, manuals, etc.
Dystopias—Fiction.
Dystopias—History.
Dystopias in literature.
    "   —Addresses, essays, lectures.
End of the world in literature.
Extrasensory perception—Fiction.
Fall of man in art.
Fall of man in literature.
Famous monsters of filmland.
Fantastic adventures—Indexes.
Fantastic drama.
Fantastic drama, English.
FANTASTIC FICTION.
    "   —Addresses, essays, lectures.

Fantastic fiction	—Authorship.
"	—Awards.
"	—Bibliography.
"	—Bibliography—Catalogs.
"	—Bibliography—First editions.
"	—Bio-bibliography.
"	—Book reviews.
"	—Book reviews—Indexes.
"	—Collectibles—Prices—United States.
"	—Congresses.
"	—Dictionaries.
"	—History and criticism.
"	—History and criticism—Addresses, essays, lectures.
"	—History and criticism—Bibliography.
"	—History and criticism—Congresses.
"	—Illustrations.
"	—Jewish authors.
"	—Miscellanea.
"	—Periodicals.
"	—Periodicals—Bibliography.
"	—Periodicals—History.
"	—Periodicals—Indexes.
"	—Stories, plots, etc.
"	—Themes, motives.
"	—Translations from Chinese.
"	—Translations from English.
"	—Translations from foreign literature.
"	—Translations from French.
"	—Translations from German.
"	—Translations from Romanian.
"	—Translations from Russian.
"	—Translations from Yiddish.
"	—Translations into English.
"	—Translations into French.
"	—Translations into German.
"	—Translations into Italian.
"	—Translations into Japanese.
"	—Translations into Japanese—Bibliography.
"	—Translations into Russian.
"	—Women authors.
"	—Women authors—History and criticism.
"	—20th century—History and criticism—Addresses, essays, lectures.
Fantastic fiction, American.	
"	—Dictionaries.

Fantastic fiction, American—Handbooks, manuals, etc.
" —History and criticism.
" —History and criticism—Addresses, essays, lectures.
" —History and criticism—Congresses.
" —Illustrations.
" —Indexes.
" —Periodicals—Indexes.
" —Stories, plots, etc.
" —Women authors—History and criticism.
Fantastic fiction, Argentine.
" —History and criticism.
Fantastic fiction, Bulgarian.
" —History and criticism.
Fantastic fiction, Canadian.
Fantastic fiction, Chinese.
" —Translations into English.
Fantastic fiction, Croatian.
" —History and criticism—Addresses, essays, lectures.
Fantastic fiction, Cuban.
Fantastic fiction, Czech.
Fantastic fiction, Dutch.
Fantastic fiction, English.
" —Bibliography.
" —Concordances.
" —Dictionaries.
" —History and criticism.
" —History and criticism—Congresses.
" —Indexes.
" —Themes, motives.
" —Translations from Chinese.
" —Translations from French.
" —Translations from Romanian.
" —Translations into French.
Fantastic fiction, French.
" —Belgium—Bibliography.
" —History and criticism.
" —Translations from English.
" —Translations into English.
Fantastic fiction, French-Canadian.
Fantastic fiction, German.
" —Austrian authors.
" —Germany (East)
" —History and criticism.
Fantastic fiction, Italian.

8

Fantastic fiction, Italian—History and criticism.
" —Translations from foreign languages.
" —20th century.
Fantastic fiction, Japanese.
" —Bibliography.
" —Translations from foreign languages—Bibliography.
Fantastic fiction, Latin American.
Fantastic fiction, Macedonian.
Fantastic fiction, Mexican.
Fantastic fiction, Nicaraguan.
Fantastic fiction, Norwegian.
Fantastic fiction, Panamanian.
Fantastic fiction, Peruvian.
Fantastic fiction, Polish.
Fantastic fiction, Romanian.
" —History and criticism.
" —Translations into English.
Fantastic fiction, Russian.
" —History and criticism.
" —History and criticism—Addresses, essays, lectures.
" —Siberia.
Fantastic fiction, Scottish.
Fantastic fiction, Spanish.
Fantastic fiction, Spanish American.
" —History and criticism.
Fantastic fiction, Yiddish.
Fantastic fiction, Yugoslav.
Fantastic four (Comic strip)
FANTASTIC FILMS.
" —Biography.
" —Catalogs.
" —Dictionaries.
" —Dictionaries—German.
" —Exhibitions.
" —History and criticism.
" —History and criticism—Addresses, essays, lectures.
" —History and criticism—Congresses.
" —History and criticism—Periodicals.
" —Periodicals.
" —Periodicals—History.
" —Plots, themes, etc.
" —Production and direction—Periodicals.
" —Religious aspects.

Fantastic four (Comic strip)
FANTASTIC LITERATURE.
    " —Addresses, essays, lectures.
    " —Awards.
    " —Bibliography.
    " —Bibliography—Methodology.
    " —Collected works.
    " —Dictionaries—German.
    " —Handbooks, manuals, etc.
    " —History and criticism.
    " —History and criticism—Congresses.
    " —History and criticism—Periodicals.
    " —Periodicals.
    " —Publishing—California.
    " —Publishing—United States—History.
    " —Statistics.
    " —Study and teaching.
Fantastic literature, American.
    " —Bibliography—Catalogs.
Fantastic literature, Bulgarian.
Fantastic literature, Czech.
    " —History and criticism.
Fantastic literature, English.
    " —Bibliography—Catalogs.
    " —History and criticism.
Fantastic literature, French.
    " —History and criticism.
Fantastic literature, Latin American.
Fantastic literature, Spanish.
Fantastic poetry.
Fantastic poetry, American.
Fantastic poetry, English.
    " —History and criticism.
Fantastic poetry, Russian.
    " —History and criticism.
Fantastic television programs.
    " —History and criticism.
    " —History and criticism—Periodicals.
    " —Plots, themes, etc.
Fantasy—Congresses.
Fantasy games.
    " —Data processing.
    " —Religious aspects—Christianity.
    " —Social aspects.
Fantasy in art.
    " —Addresses, essays, lectures.

Fantasy in art	—Catalogs.
"	—Congresses.
"	—Dictionaries.
"	—Dictionaries—German.
"	—Europe.
"	—Exhibitions.
"	—France.
"	—Japan—Exhibitions.
"	—Themes, motives—Addresses, essays, lectures.
"	—United States—Exhibitions.
Fantasy in literature.	
"	—Addresses, essays, lectures.
"	—Congresses.
Fantasy in mass media.	
"	—Bibliography.
"	—United States.
Fanzines.	
"	—Directories.
"	—Indexes.
Frankenstein (Fictitious character)	
"	—Catalogs.
"	—Drama.
Frankenstein films.	
"	—Catalogs.
"	—Plots, themes, etc.
Future in literature.	
"	—Bibliography.
Future in popular culture.	
"	—History.
"	—United States—History—20th century—Exhibitions.
Future life—Fiction.	
Future life in literature.	
Futurian Society of New York.	
Futurism (Literary movement)	
"	—History and criticism.
"	—Italy.
"	—Italy—History.
"	—Italy—History and criticism.
"	—Latin America.
"	—Soviet Union.
"	—Soviet Union—Addresses, essays, lectures.
G-8 (Fictitious character)	
Geographical myths.	
"	—Addresses, essays, lectures.
"	—Angola.

Geographical myths   —Anecdotes, facetiae, satire, etc.
"   —Maps—Exhibitions.
Geographical myths, Irish.
Geographical myths in art.
"   —Exhibitions.
Geographical myths in literature.
"   —Illustrations.
Geographical myths in mass media.
Ghost plays.
Ghost plays, Japanese.
GHOST STORIES. [includes fiction and nonfiction]
"   —Bibliography.
"   —History and criticism.
"   —History and criticism—Addresses, essays, lectures.
"   —Indexes.
"   —Juvenile fiction.
"   —Juvenile literature.
"   —Translations from Chinese.
"   —Translations from English.
"   —Translations from French.
"   —Translations into English.
"   —Translations into German.
"   —Translations into Japanese.
Ghost stories, Afrikaans.
Ghost stories, American.
"   —Alabama.
"   —History and criticism—Addresses, essays, lectures.
"   —Kentucky.
"   —Maryland—Frederick County.
"   —Pennsylvania—Chester County.
Ghost stories, Burmese.
Ghost stories, Canadian.
Ghost stories, Chinese.
Ghost stories, Dutch.
Ghost stories, English.
"   —Cornwall.
"   —History and criticism.
Ghost stories, French.
Ghost stories, German.
"   —Prussia, East.
Ghost stories, Icelandic.
Ghost stories, Irish.
Ghost stories, Italian.
Ghost stories, Japanese.

Ghost stories, Japanese—Japan—Okayama (Prefecture)
Ghost stories, Korean.
Ghost stories, Marathi.
Ghost stories, Norwegian.
Ghost stories, Scottish.
Ghost stories, South African.
Ghost stories, Thai.
Ghosts—Fiction.
Ghosts—Literary collections.
Ghosts in art.
Ghosts in literature.
Ghouls and ogres. [includes fiction and nonfiction]
" —Anecdotes, facetiae, satire, etc.
" —Fiction.
" —Juvenile literature.
Godzilla films.
Golem.
" —Juvenile literature.
Gothic literature.
Gothic revival (Literature)
" —Addresses, essays, lectures.
" —Bibliography.
" —England.
" —Germany.
" —History and criticism.
" —Italy—History and criticism—Addresses, essays, lectures.
" —Portugal.
" —Portugal—Bibliography.
Halloween—Fiction.
Halloween—Juvenile literature.
Halloween—Juvenile poetry.
Heroes unlimited (Game)
High fantasy (Game)
History—Errors, inventions, etc.
Horror—Literary collections.
Horror—Periodicals.
Horror comics.
Horror films.
" —Addresses, essays, lectures.
" —Biography.
" —Catalogs.
" —Dictionaries.
" —Dictionaries—German.
" —Great Britain—Plots, themes, etc.
" —History and criticism.

Horror films	—History and criticism—Addresses, essays, lectures.
"	—History and criticism—Juvenile literature.
"	—History and criticism—Periodicals.
"	—Hungary.
"	—Juvenile literature.
"	—Plots, themes, etc.
"	—Poetry.
"	—Production and direction—Juvenile literature.
"	—Psychological aspects.
"	—Quizzes.
"	—United States—History and criticism.
Horror in art.	
"	—Exhibitions.
Horror in literature.	
Horror in mass media.	
"	—Addresses, essays, lectures.
"	—Bibliography.
Horror plays.	
Horror plays, American.	
Horror radio programs.	
"	—Dictionaries.
Horror stories. [cancelled]	
HORROR TALES.	
"	—Addresses, essays, lectures.
"	—Authorship.
"	—Bibliography.
"	—Bibliography—Catalogs.
"	—Bio-bibliography.
"	—Dictionaries.
"	—History and criticism.
"	—Illustrations.
"	—Periodicals.
"	—Stories, plots, etc.
"	—Translations from English.
"	—Translations from foreign literature.
"	—Translations from French.
"	—Translations from Spanish.
"	—Translations into Czech.
"	—Translations into English.
"	—Translations into German.
"	—Translations into Hungarian.
"	—Translations into Italian.
"	—Translations into Spanish.
"	—Translations into Swedish.
"	—Women authors.

Horror tales, American.
      "   —Bibliography.
      "   —Hawaii.
      "   —History and criticism.
      "   —History and criticism—Addresses, essays, lectures.
      "   —History and criticism—Bibliography.
      "   —Women authors.
      "   —20th century.
Horror tales, Australian.
Horror tales, Canadian.
Horror tales, Czech.
Horror tales, Dutch.
Horror tales, English.
      "   —Bibliography.
      "   —Bibliography—First editions.
      "   —History and criticism.
      "   —History and criticism—Addresses, essays, lectures.
      "   —History and criticism—Bibliography.
      "   —Translations from French.
      "   —Women authors.
Horror tales, Finnish.
Horror tales, French.
      "   —Translations into English.
Horror tales, German.
Horror tales, Hungarian.
Horror tales, Italian.
Horror tales, Japanese.
      "   —Japan—Tohoku region.
Horror tales, Korean.
Horror tales, Mauritian (English)
Horror tales, Philippine (English)
Horror tales, Russian.
      "   —History and criticism.
Horror tales, Spanish.
      "   —Spain—Andalusia.
Horror tales, Swedish.
Horror television programs.
      "   —Dictionaries.
Imaginary books and libraries.
      "   —Exhibitions.
      "   —Reviews.
Imaginary languages in literature.
Imaginary revolutions.
Imaginary societies.

Imaginary societies—Illustrations.
Imagination in literature.
Interplanetary voyages—Juvenile literature. [includes nonfiction]
Interplanetary voyages—Literary collections. [includes nonfiction]
Interplanetary voyages—Poetry.
Interstellar travel. [includes some nonfiction]
Life on other planets—Anecdotes, facetiae, satire, etc.
Life on other planets—Fiction.
Literature and science.
Literature and technology.
Logan (Fictitious character)
Magic in art.
Magic in literature.
    "   —Addresses, essays, lectures.
Magic realism (Art)
Magic realism (Literature)
Magicians—Fiction.
Mars (Planet)—Fiction.
Mars (Planet)—Juvenile literature.
Mars (Planet)—Stories.
Marvelous, The, in literature.
    "   —Addresses, essays, lectures.
    "   —Collected works.
Melusine (Legendary character) in literature.
Metamorphosis in art.
Metamorphosis in literature.
    "   —Congresses.
Middle Earth (Imaginary place)—Maps.
Monsters in art.
Monsters in literature.
    "   —Addresses, essays, lectures.
    "   —Bibliography.
    "   —Congresses.
Monsters in mass media.
    "   —Catalogs.
    "   —Juvenile literature.
Monsters in motion pictures.
Moon—Literary collections.
Moon in art.
Moon in literature.
Moving-pictures—Plots, themes, etc.—Horror. [cancelled]
Moving-pictures—Plots, themes, etc.—Science fiction. [cancelled]
Mummies—Fiction.
Nuclear warfare—Fiction.
Occult sciences in literature.
Occultism in art.

Occultism in literature.
" —Addresses, essays, lectures.
Outer space—Posters.
Palladium (Game)
Penny dreadfuls.
" —Bibliography—Exhibitions.
Rhodan, Perry (Fictitious character)
Robinsonades.
Robots—Fiction.
Robots in literature.
Russian language—Readers (Science fiction)
SCIENCE FICTION.
" —Addresses, essays, lectures.
" —Anecdotes, facetiae, satire, etc.
" —Authorship.
" —Authorship—Addresses, essays, lectures.
" —Awards.
" —Bibliography.
" —Bibliography—Catalogs.
" —Bibliography—First editions.
" —Bibliography—Methodology.
" —Bibliography—Periodicals.
" —Bibliography—Union lists.
" —Bio-bibliography.
" —Book reviews.
" —Book reviews—Catalogs.
" —Book reviews—Indexes.
" —Book reviews—Periodicals.
" —Caricatures and cartoons.
" —Collected works.
" —Collectibles.
" —Collectibles—United States—Catalogs.
" —Collections.
" —Collectors and collecting.
" —Comic books, strips, etc.
" —Comic books, strips, etc.—History and criticism.
" —Congresses.
" —Dictionaries.
" —Dictionaries—French.
" —Dictionaries—German.
" —Dictionaries—Italian.
" —Dictionaries, indexes, etc.
" —Exhibitions.
" —Handbooks, manuals, etc.
" —History.

Science fiction	—History and criticism.
"	—History and criticism—Addresses, essays, lectures.
"	—History and criticism—Bibliography.
"	—History and criticism—Bibliography—Catalogs.
"	—History and criticism—Catalogs.
"	—History and criticism—Handbooks, manuals, etc.
"	—History and criticism—Indexes.
"	—History and criticism—Indexes—Periodicals.
"	—History and criticism—Juvenile literature.
"	—History and criticism—Miscellanea.
"	—History and criticism—Periodicals.
"	—History and criticism—Theory, etc.
"	—Illustrations.
"	—Illustrations—Catalogs.
"	—Illustrations—Exhibitions.
"	—Illustrations—Juvenile literature.
"	—Indexes.
"	—Indexes—Periodicals.
"	—Jewish authors.
"	—Juvenile literature.
"	—Juvenile literature—Bibliography.
"	—Library resources.
"	—Library resources—Canada.
"	—Library resources—United States.
"	—Miscellanea.
"	—Outlines, syllabi, etc.
"	—Periodicals.
"	—Periodicals—Bibliography.
"	—Periodicals—History.
"	—Periodicals—Indexes.
"	—Poetry.
"	—Psychological aspects.
"	—Public opinion.
"	—Publishing—Addresses, essays, lectures.
"	—Publishing—California.
"	—Publishing—Great Britain—History—20th century.
"	—Publishing—United States—History.
"	—Readers.
"	—Religious aspects.
"	—Religious aspects—Addresses, essays, lectures.
"	—Religious aspects—Buddhism.
"	—Religious aspects—Christianity.
"	—Social aspects.

Science fiction	—Societies, etc.
"	—Statistics.
"	—Stories, plots, etc.
"	—Study and teaching.
"	—Study and teaching—Addresses, essays, lectures.
"	—Study and teaching—France—Addresses, essays, lectures.
"	—Technique.
"	—Technique—Addresses, essays, lectures.
"	—Terminology.
"	—Translations from Czech.
"	—Translations from English.
"	—Translations from foreign languages—Bibliography.
"	—Translations from foreign literature.
"	—Translations from foreign literature—Bibliography.
"	—Translations from French.
"	—Translations from Japanese.
"	—Translations from Polish.
"	—Translations from Romanian.
"	—Translations from Russian.
"	—Translations from Russian—Bibliography.
"	—Translations from Slovak.
"	—Translations into Danish.
"	—Translations into Danish—Bibliography.
"	—Translations into English.
"	—Translations into foreign languages.
"	—Translations into foreign languages—Bibliography.
"	—Translations into French.
"	—Translations into German.
"	—Translations into Italian.
"	—Translations into Italian—Bibliography.
"	—Translations into Japanese—Bibliography.
"	—Translations into Korean.
"	—Translations into Lithuanian.
"	—Translations into Norwegian.
"	—Translations into Polish.
"	—Translations into Russian.
"	—Translations into Serbo-Croatian.
"	—Translations into Spanish.
"	—Women authors.
"	—Women authors—Bibliography.
"	—Women authors—History and criticism—

Science fiction Addresses, essays, lectures.
    —Yearbooks.
" —20th century—History and criticism—
    Addresses, essays, lectures.
Science fiction, American.
" —Bibliography.
" —Bio-bibliography.
" —Dictionaries.
" —Dictionaries, indexes, etc.
" —Handbooks, manuals, etc.
" —History and criticism.
" —History and criticism—Addresses, essays,
    lectures.
" —History and criticism—Congresses.
" —Indexes.
" —Periodicals—Indexes.
" —Stories, plots, etc.
" —Translations into German.
" —Translations into Spanish.
" —Women authors.
" —Women authors—Bibliography.
" —Women authors—History and criticism.
" —Women authors—Translations into French.
Science fiction, Argentine.
Science fiction, Australian.
Science fiction, Brazilian.
" —History and criticism.
Science fiction, Bulgarian.
Science fiction, Canadian.
Science fiction, Chinese.
" —History and criticism—Addresses, essays,
    lectures.
Science fiction, Cuban.
Science fiction, Czech.
" —History and criticism.
Science fiction, Danish.
Science fiction, Dutch.
Science fiction, East European.
Science fiction, English.
" —Bibliography.
" —Bio-bibliography.
" —History and criticism.
" —History and criticism—Addresses, essays,
    lectures.
" —History and criticism—Congresses.
" —Indexes.

Science fiction, English	—Singapore authors.
"	—Stories, plots, etc.
"	—Translations from French.
"	—Translations from Russian.
"	—Translations from Ukrainian.
"	—Translations into German.
"	—Women authors.
"	—Women authors—Bibliography.

Science fiction, Flemish.
Science fiction, French.
"	—Exhibitions.
"	—History and criticism.
"	—History and criticism—Juvenile literature.
"	—Translations from English.
"	—Translations into English.

Science fiction, French-Canadian.
Science fiction, German.
"	—Aargau.
"	—Dictionaries—German.
"	—German (East)—History and criticism.
"	—History and criticism.
"	—Translations from English.

Science fiction, Italian.
| " | —Translations from foreign languages. |

Science fiction, Japanese.
"	—Bibliography.
"	—History and criticism.
"	—Translations from foreign languages—Bibliography.

Science fiction, Jewish.
Science fiction, Latin American.
Science fiction, Lithuanian.
Science fiction, Mexican.
Science fiction, Norwegian.
Science fiction, Peruvian.
Science fiction, Polish.
Science fiction, Romanian.
| " | —Craiova. |
| " | —Translations from foreign languages. |

Science fiction, Russian.
"	—History and criticism.
"	—History and criticism—Addresses, essays, lectures.
"	—Translations into English.

Science fiction, Salvadorian.
Science fiction, Singapore (English)

Science fiction, Slavic.
" —History and criticism—Addresses, essays, lectures.
Science fiction, Slovak.
Science fiction, Slovenian.
Science fiction, Spanish.
Science fiction, Thai.
Science fiction, Ukrainian.
" —Translations into English.
Science fiction films.
" —Addresses, essays, lectures.
" —Catalogs.
" —Dictionaries.
" —Dictionaries—German.
" —History and criticism.
" —History and criticism—Addresses, essays, lectures.
" —History and criticism—Juvenile literature.
" —History and criticism—Miscellanea.
" —Periodicals.
" —Pictorial works.
" —Plots, themes, etc.
" —Psychological aspects.
" —Religious aspects.
" —Reviews.
" —United States—History and criticism.
" —United States—Plots, themes, etc.
Science Fiction Foundation.
Science fiction illustrators.
Science fiction in art.
Science fiction plays.
Science fiction plays, American.
Science fiction poetry, American.
Science fiction television programs.
" —Dictionaries.
Scientists—Fiction.
Sorcery (Game)
Space and time in art.
" —Addresses, essays, lectures.
Space and time in literature.
" —Addresses, essays, lectures.
" —Congresses.
Space flight in literature.
" —Bibliography.
Spider (Fictitious character)
Star trek (Motion picture)—Collectibles.

Star trek (Television program)—Collectibles.
Star trek II, the wrath of Khan (Motion picture)—Collectibles.
Star trek films.
       "   —Collectibles.
Star wars films.
       "   —Collectibles.
       "   —Juvenile literature.
Startling stories—Indexes.
Stoker, Bram, 1847-1912—Characters—Count Dracula.
Subject headings—Fantastic literature.
Subject headings—Science fiction.
Superman (Comic strip)
Superman films.
Superman in literature.
Superman in mass media.
Supernatural—Comic books, strips, etc.
Supernatural—Fiction.
Supernatural—Juvenile fiction.
Supernatural—Poetry.
Supernatural—Poetry—Bibliography.
Supernatural in literature.
       "   —Addresses, essays, lectures.
       "   —Bibliography.
Supernatural in moving-pictures.
       "   —Miscellanea.
Tarzan (Fictitious character)
Tarzan (Fictitious character) in mass media.
Tarzan films.
Tarzan in literature.
Tarzan in mass media.
Time in art.
       "   —Exhibitions.
Time in literature.
       "   —Addresses, essays, lectures.
Time in motion pictures.
Traveller (Game)
Twenty-first century—Forecasts. [includes some nonfiction]
Utopias. [includes some nonfiction]
Utopias in literature.
       "   —Addresses, essays, lectures.
       "   —Bibliography—Catalogs.
       "   —Congresses.
       "   —History.
Vampire films.
       "   —History and criticism.
       "   —History and criticism—Juvenile literature.

Vampires—Bibliography.
Vampires—Fiction.
Vampires—Juvenile humor.
Vampires—Literary collections.
Vampires—Poetry.
Vampires—Stories.
Vampires in literature.
" —Addresses, essays, lectures.
" —Bibliography.
" —Literary collections.
Voodooism—Fiction.
Voodooism in art.
Voyages, Imaginary.
" —Bibliography.
" —Bibliography—Catalogs.
" —Caricatures and cartoons.
" —Congresses.
" —Early works to 1800.
" —Exhibitions.
" —History and criticism.
" —Irish.
" —Juvenile fiction.
" —Juvenile literature.
" —Maps—Exhibitions.
Voyages, Imaginary, in mass media.
Voyages to the otherworld. [includes some nonfiction]
Voyages to the otherworld in literature.
Wargames.
" —Juvenile literature.
Weird tales.
" —Indexes.
Werewolf films.
Werewolves—Drama.
Werewolves—Fiction.
Werewolves—Juvenile Literature.
Werwolf films. [cancelled]
Werwolves—Fiction. [cancelled]
Witchcraft in art.
Witchcraft in literature.
" —Addresses, essays, lectures.
World War III. [includes some nonfiction]
" —Anecdotes, facetiae, satire, etc.
" —Humor, caricatures, etc.
" —Poetry.

STANDARD SUBDIVISIONS FOR AUTHORS

I use as an example Edgar Rice Burroughs, although the headings listed below have not necessarily been applied to his name, and are intended only to provide samples for application elsewhere.

Burroughs, Edgar Rice, 1875-1950.
" —Allusions.
" —Bibliography.
" —Bibliography—First editions.
" —Bibliography—Indexes.
" —Biography.
" —Biography—Marriage.
" —Characters.
" —Characters—Tarzan.
" —Characters—Tarzan—Addresses, essays, lectures.
" —Characters—Tarzan—Bibliography.
" —Characters—Tarzan—Pictorial works.
" —Correspondence.
" —Criticism and interpretation.
" —Dictionaries, indexes, etc.
" —Film adaptations.
" —Friends and associates.
" —In fiction, drama, poetry, etc.
" —Indexes.
" —Influence.
" —Influence—Bibliography.
" —Influence—Philip José Farmer.
" —Journeys—England.
" —Juvenile literature.
" —Knowledge—Medicine.
" —Language.
" —Miscellanea.
" —Parodies, imitations, etc.
" —Plots.
" —Quotations.
" —Settings.
" —Societies, etc.
" —Sources.
" —Style.

Similar subdivisions may be used with fictitious characters:

Tarzan (Fictitious character)
" —Addresses, essays, lectures.
" —Bibliography.
" —Bibliography—First editions.
" —Bibliography—Indexes.
" —Dictionaries.
" —Drama.
" —Fiction.
" —Juvenile fiction.
" —Library.
" —Name.
" —Pictorial works.
" —Poetry.
" —Societies, etc.

II
CLASSIFICATION NUMBERS

INTRODUCTION

This section is arranged by classification number, with an index of subjects at the end. The Library of Congress classes criticism and anthologies into their respective national literatures, or, if none predominates, into PN (general literature). Most of the numbers listed herein consist of two parts, general classification plus subject cutter (which is immutable); to these must be added a first or second cutter (for main entry), and a publication date. Note that anthologies are established under title main entries, with added entries for their editors. Thus, a 1987 anthology of American science fiction stories entitled *Far Out* might be classed in PS648.S3F37 1987.

General criticism of science fiction and fantasy is classed in PN3433-3433.8, specific criticism of national literatures being classed into their respective tables (PS374.S35 for American science fiction, PR830.S35 for British, etc.). Anthologies are similarly classed into PN6071.S33/PN6120.95.S33, PS648.S3, and PR1309.S3, respectively. Most SF anthologies with even half of their stories by American writers are actually classed into PS648.S3. Collections of stories by one author are classed with that author's literature number, as is criticism on a specific writer. Criticism on two writers is classed under the first author's literature number; criticism on three or more authors is considered general or national criticism. There is no consistency in the assignment of subject cutters in the various national literatures—for science fiction, for example, one can find any range from S26-S42. Similarly, there is no consistency in the development of appropriate subject headings, which LC generates as needed.

CLASS G (GEOGRAPHY)

Atlases of imaginary, literary, and mythological regions, etc., A-Z

G3122 .M5 Middle Earth

CLASS GV (SPORTS AND GAMES)

Games and amusements. Games not otherwise provided for, A-Z

    GV1202   .F35   Fantasy games [cancelled—see below]
                     .H54   High fantasy (Game) [cancelled—see below]

Fantasy games

  General works

  GV1469.6

  Individual games, A-Z

    GV1469.62   .D84   Dungeons and dragons
                         .H45   Heroes unlimited
                         .H54   High fantasy
                         .P34   Palladium
                         .S65   Sorcery

CLASS HX

Utopia. The ideal state. Particular works.
  HX810   Collections
  HX811   Individual works. By date of first edition

CLASS N (ART)

Visual arts. Special subjects of art. Other special topics, A-Z

    N8217   .F28   Fantasy
               .G8   Grotesque
               .H68   Horror

DRAWING. DESIGN. ILLUSTRATION.

Special subjects. Other, A-Z

    NC825   .S34

Drawing for reproduction. Illustration. Special subjects, A-Z

    NC961.7   .A53   Androids

```
         .R6    Rockets
         .S34   Science fiction
         .S58   Space vehicles
```

Periodical illustration. Special subjects, A-Z

```
NC968.5  .H6    Horror tales
         .S33   Science fiction
```

Book jackets. Phonorecord jackets. Special subjects, A-Z

```
NC1882.7 .S35   Science fiction
```

Posters. Special topics, A-Z

```
NC1849   .S63   Outer space posters
```

Painting. Special subjects. Other subjects. Miscellaneous, A-Z

```
ND1460   .F35   Fantasy
```

The Arts. Special subjects, A-Z

```
NX650    .F36   Fantasy
         .S3    Science fiction
```

CLASS P (LANGUAGES AND LITERATURE)

Communication. Mass Media. Special aspects. Other, A-Z

```
P96      .F36           Fantasy
         .F362.U66+     Fantasy—United States
         .G46           Geographical myths
         .H46           Heroes
         .H65           Horror
         .M6            Monsters
         .S34           Science fiction
         .S94           Superman
         .T37           Tarzan
         .V68           Voyages, Imaginary
```

CLASS PC (ROMANIAN LITERATURE)

Collections. Prose. Special topics, A-Z. [anthologies]

```
PC838.5  .S3    Science fiction
```

CLASS PG (SLAVIC LANGUAGES AND LITERATURE)

Russian literature. History. By period. 20th century. Revolutionary epoch. Soviet literature. Special topics, A-Z

    PG3026   .S35   Science fiction

Special forms. Prose fiction. Special topics and subjects, A-Z. [criticism]

    PG3096   .U94   Utopias

Special forms of literature. Prose fiction. Special kinds of fiction. Other, A-Z. [criticism]

    PG3098   .H67   Horror tales
                      .S5   Science fiction

Folk literature. History and criticism. Special forms. Popular poetry. Special types. Byliny. Special topics, A-Z

    PG3104.2   .F3   Fantastic poetry

CLASS PJ (SEMITIC LANGUAGES AND LITERATURES)

Arabic literature. History and criticism. Treatment of special subjects, A-Z

    PJ7519   .U85   Utopias

CLASS PL (ORIENTAL LANGUAGES AND LITERATURES)

JAPANESE LITERATURE

History and criticism. Special aspects and topics. Treatment of special subjects, A-Z

    PL721   .F27   Fantastic fiction
                  .S3   Science fiction
                  .S8   Supernatural

History. Prose. Fiction. Special forms, A-Z

    PL740.65   .S3   Science fiction

CHINESE LITERATURE

History. Special aspects and topics. Treatment of special subjects, A-Z

    PL2275   .G45   Ghosts

History. Special forms. Fiction. Special topics, A-Z

    PL2419   .G5   Ghost stories

Collections. Fiction. Special topics, A-Z

    PL2629   .F35   Fantastic fiction
                       .G5   Ghost stories
                       .S34   Science fiction

CLASS PN (GENERAL LITERATURE)

Theory. Philosophy. Esthetics.
General Special. Relation to and treatment of special elements and subjects. Other special topics, A-Z. Class here works that are not limited to one form, nor to one national literature.

    PN56   .A5   Allegory
                     .A8   Astronautics
                     .A82   Astronomy
                     .A9   Automata [robots]
                     .C68   Cosmology
                     .E63   End of the world
                     .F29   Fall of man
                     .F34   Fantastic literature
                     .F8   Futurism
                     .G7   Grotesque
                     .H6   Horror
                     .M24   Magic realism
                     .M3   The marvelous, miracles, wonders, etc.
                     .M52   Mesmerism
                     .M53   Metamorphosis
                     .M55   Monsters
                     .M94   Myth
                     .M95   Mythology
                     .O33   Occultism. Occult sciences
                     .O7   Otherworld
                     .P744 Prophecies
                     .S667 Space

.S735	Stars
.S8	Supernatural
.S87	Surrealism
.T5	Time
.U8	Utopias
.V3	Vampires
.V59	Voyages, Imaginary
.V6	Voyages, Interplanetary
.W37	Water spirits
.W49	Witchcraft

Characters. Special classes of people, A-Z

PN56.5   Sprites

Individual characters, A-Z

PN57	.A6	Arthur and Arthurian legends
	.D4	Devil
	.F3	Faust
	.F6	Flying Dutchman
	.G56	Golem
	.M77	Munchausen
	.P25	Pan (Deity)
	.S94	The superman
	.U5	Undine
	.W3	Wandering Jew

Drama. Philosophy, esthetics, scope, relations, etc. Relations to, and treatment of, special subjects. Other special, A-Z

PN1650	.A42	Alchemy
	.G7	Grotesque
	.T5	Time

Broadcasting. Television broadcasting. Special Topics. Other special topics, A-Z

PN1992.8   .F35   Fantastic television programs

Motion Pictures. Special topics, A-Z

PN1995.9	.A3	Adventure films
	.F36	Fantastic films
	.F8	Frankenstein films
	.G63	Godzilla films

.H6	Horror films
.M6	Monster films
.M97	Mythology [in films]
.S26	Science fiction films
.S694	Star trek films
.S77	Superman films
.S8	Supernatural [in films]
.S85	Surrealism [in films]
.T3	Tarzan films
.T55	Time [in films]
.V3	Vampire films
.W38	Werewolf films

PROSE. PROSE FICTION. [Criticism]

Philosophy, theory, etc. Relation to and treatment of special subjects. Other special, A-z

PN3352	.N83	Nuclear warfare

Technique. Authorship. Special forms, subjects, etc. Other, A-Z

PN3377.5	.F34	Fantastic fiction
	.H67	Horror tales
	.S3	Science fiction

Special kinds of fiction.

PN3432	Robinsonades, "avanturiers," etc.

Science fiction

PN3433	Periodicals, societies, etc.
PN3433.2	Congresses
PN3433.3	Exhibitions, museums, etc.
PN3433.4	Encyclopedias. Dictionaries
PN3433.5	General works
PN3433.6	Special topics (not A-Z)
PN3433.7	Study and teaching
PN3433.8	History
PN3435	Fantastic fiction. Tales of wonder, terror, etc.
PN3437	Fairy tales

Other kinds of fiction, A-Z

PN3448	.S45	Science fiction [cancelled in favor of PN3433]
	.U7	Utopian literature

Journalism. United States. Special topics. Pulp magazines, A-Z

PN4878.5	.S6	Spider

Other special topics, A-Z

PN4888	.S77	Supernatural

COLLECTIONS [anthologies]

Collections of general literature. By subject, A-Z. [anthologies]

PN6071	.A78	Apocalyptic literature
	.A84	Arthurian romances. King Arthur
	.A94	Automata [robots]
	.C76	Cosmogony
	.D4	Death
	.D47	Devil
	.E5	End of the world
	.F15	Fairy tales. Fairies
	.F25	Fantastic fiction
	.F28	Fate and fatalism
	.F33	Faust
	.F86	Future life
	.G45	Ghost stories
	.G6	Golem
	.H4	Heroes
	.H727	Horror tales
	.I64	Interplanetary voyages
	.J5	Jewish legends and tales
	.L35	Lazarus
	.M155	Magic
	.M17	Man, Primitive
	.M25	The marvelous
	.M54	Miracles
	.M6	Moon
	.M77	Mummies
	.O22	Occult sciences
	.P27	Parables
	.S2	Satanism
	.S33	Science fiction
	.S58	Space flight to the Moon
	.S67	Stars

	.S9	Supernatural
	.T5	Time
	.V3	Vampires

Poetry. Special. By subject or form, A-Z

PN6110	.D4	Death and immortality
	.F3	Fairies
	.F33	Fantastic poetry
	.G5	Ghosts
	.G52	Giants
	.H17	Heaven
	.M6	Moon
	.M8	Mythology
	.S75	Stars
	.S87	Sun
	.S9	Supernatural
	.T5	Terrer and wonder
	.V37	Vampires

Drama. Special. By subject or form, A-Z

PN6120	.E9	Everyman
	.F33	Faust
	.G45	Ghost plays

Fiction. Special. By subject or form, A-Z. [anthologies]

PN6120.95	.F25	Fantastic fiction
	.G45	Ghost stories
	.H727	Horror tales
	.S33	Science fiction
	.V3	Vampires

Wit and humor. Special topics, A-Z. [anthologies]

PN6231	.A73	Astrology
	.C85	Curiosities and wonders
	.D35	Death
	.F283	Fairies
	.G45	Ghosts
	.G47	Ghouls and ogres
	.G84	Gravity
	.M665	Monsters
	.S42	Science fiction
	.S645	Space travel. Outer space

	.S88	Superstition
	.T64	Time
	.U54	Unicorns
	.V27	Vampires

CLASS PQ (ROMANCE LITERATURES)

FRENCH LITERATURE

History. Special subjects and classes, A-Z

PQ145.1	.D33	Death
	.F32	Fantastic fiction

Prose and prose fiction. Special. Prose fiction. Special topics, A-Z

PQ637	.F27	Fairy tales
	.F3	Fantastic fiction
	.M98	Myth
	.S34	Science fiction
	.S65	Space and time
	.V7	Voyages, Imaginary

Collections. General. Special topics, A-Z

PQ1110	.F3	Fantastic literature

Prose. Prose fiction. Special forms and subjects, A-Z

PQ1276	.F3	Fantastic fiction
	.S35	Science fiction

ITALIAN LITERATURE

History and criticism. Special subjects, A-Z

PQ4053	.A7	Arthurian legends
	.S25	Science fiction

Literary history and criticism. Prose. Special topics, A-Z

PQ4181	.F36	Fantastic fiction
	.S35	Science fiction

Collections. Prose. By subject, A-Z

    PQ4249.6   .F34   Fantastic fiction

SPANISH LITERATURE

Literary history and criticism. Prose. Special topics, A-Z

    PQ6147   .S32   Science fiction

History. Prose. Prose fiction. Special topics, A-Z

    PQ6256   .F35   Fantastic fiction
                      .S34   Science fiction

MEXICAN LITERATURE

History and criticism. Prose. Fiction. History. Special topics, A-Z

    PQ7207   .F27   Fantastic fiction

ARGENTINIAN LITERATURE

History and criticism. Prose. Fiction. History. Special topics, A-Z

    PQ7707   .F27   Fantastic fiction

CLASS PR (ENGLISH LITERATURE)

CRITICISM OF ENGLISH LITERATURE

History. Special topics not limited to, or identified with, one period or form. Treatment of special subjects

    PR147   The supernatural

Other, A-Z

    PR149   .A635 Allegory
                      .A79   Arthurian romances
                      .A798 Astrology
                      .A8   Astronomy

	.D47	Devil
	.F3	Fairies
	.I58	Incubi
	.M65	Monsters
	.M95	Mythology
	.U8	Utopias

History of English literature. By period. Modern. Special topics, A-Z

PR408	.A4	Allegory
	.A7	Arthurian romances
	.F34	Fantastic literature
	.G68	Gothic literature
	.S85	Surrealism

Treatment of special subjects, A-Z

PR409	.G56	Ghosts
	.G7	Grotesque
	.H45	Heroes
	.M9	Mythology
	.O28	Occultism
	.P33	Paradise
	.V34	Vampires
	.W57	Witchcraft

By period. Elizabethan Era (1550-1640). Treatment of special subjects, A-Z

PR429	.A35	Alchemy
	.D418	Death
	.G76	Grotesque
	.W57	Witchcraft

18th century. Treatment of special subjects, A-Z

PR448	.G6	Gothic literature
	.S69	Space and time

19th century. Special topics, A-Z

PR468	.F35	Fantastic literature

19th century. Treatment of special subjects, A-Z

PR469	.V35	Vampires

20th century. Special topics, A-Z

PR478	.F35	Fantastic literature
	.M96	Myth

20th century. Treatment of special subjects, A-Z

PR479	.L35	Labyrinths

Poetry. Special topics. Other, A-Z

PR508	.D8	Dreams
	.F34	Fairies
	.M87	Myth
	.M9	Mythology
	.S65	Space

Special forms, A-Z

PR509	.M92	Myth
	.S33	Science

By period. [General table]
Special topics, A-Z

(5)	.A4	Allegory
	.I65	Immortality
	.M9	Mysticism
	.S85	Supernatural

Drama. By period. Medieval. 16th century. Special topics, A-Z

PR658	.A8	Astrology
	.D4	Death
	.H42	Heroes
	.M27	Magic
	.W58	Witchcraft

Prose. Special topics, A-Z

PR756	.U86	Utopias

By form. Prose fiction. The novel. Special topics. Other topics, A-Z. [criticism]

PR830	.A76	Arthurian romances
	.D37	Death
	.D96	Dystopias
	.E93	Evolution
	.F27	Fairy tales
	.F3	Fantastic fiction
	.F35	Fate and fatalism
	.G45	Ghost stories
	.G7	Grotesque
	.O33	Occultism
	.S35	Science fiction
	.S65	Primitive society
	.S85	Supernatural
	.T3	Tales of terror. Gothic tales
	.T5	Time
	.U7	Utopias
	.V6	Imaginary voyages

By period. 18th century. Special topics, A-Z

PR858	.H4	Heroes and heroines

19th century. Special topics, A-Z

PR868	.F3	Fantastic fiction

Victorian period. Special topics, A-Z

PR878	.S35	Science fiction

20th century. Special topics, A-Z

PR888	.A76	Avalon
	.D96	Dystopias
	.F3	Fantastic fiction
	.U7	Utopias

COLLECTIONS OF ENGLISH LITERATURE. [anthologies]

General collections. Special topics (prose and verse), A-Z

PR1111	.D7	Dreams
	.F27	Fall of man
	.G48	Ghosts
	.G67	Gothic revival
	.G7	Grotesque

| | .M55 | Monsters |
| | .S78 | Supernatural |

Poetry. Special forms and subjects. Other, by subject, A-Z

PR1195	.F34	Fairies
	.F343	Fairy tales
	.F36	Fantastic poetry
	.G47	Ghosts
	.M6	Monsters
	.S65	Soul
	.S87	Surrealism

Prose (General). Special subjects and forms, A-Z

PR1309	.E85	Extrasensory perception
	.F26	Fairy tales
	.F3	Fantastic fiction
	.G5	Ghost stories
	.H6	Horror tales
	.P45	Penny dreadfuls
	.S3	Science fiction
	.V36	Vampires
	.V4	Venus (Planet)
	.W5	Witchcraft

CANADIAN LITERATURE

History and criticism. Prose fiction. Special topics, A-Z

| PR9191.6 | .S34 | Science fiction |

Collections. General. Special topics, A-Z

| PR9194.52 | .F36 | Fantastic fiction |

Collections. Prose. Fiction. Special, by form or subject, A-Z

| PR9197.35 | .F35 | Fantastic fiction |
| | .S33 | Science fiction |

AUSTRALIAN LITERATURE

History and criticism. Prose fiction. Special topics, A-Z

PR9612.6 .S34 Science fiction

Collections. Prose. Fiction. By form or subject, A-Z

PR9617.35 S33 Science fiction

CLASS PS (AMERICAN LITERATURE)

CRITICISM OF AMERICAN LITERATURE

History. Treatment of special subjects. Other, A-Z

PS169 .A66 Apocalyptic literature
 .D47 Devil
 .E53 End of the world
 .F64 Folklore
 .G66 Good and evil
 .M88 Myth
 .T5 Time
 .U85 Utopias

By period. 19th century. Special topics, A-Z

PS217 .U8 Utopias
 .W5 Witchcraft

20th century. Special topics, A-Z

PS228 .F35 Fantastic literature
 .M9 Mythology
 .O96 Outer space

Special forms. Poetry. Special topics, A-Z

PS310 .M37 Metamorphosis
 .M96 Myth
 .N66 Nothingness

Prose. Prose fiction. Special forms and topics, A-Z. [criticism]

PS374 .A45 Allegory
 .A65 Apocalypse
 .A78 Arthurian romances
 .C9 Cybernetics
 .D5 Dime novels

.D96	Dystopias
.F26	Fall of man
.F27	Fantastic fiction
.F86	Future
.G68	Gothic revival
.H67	Horror tales
.M52	Millennialism
.M88	Myth
.Q47	Quests
.S35	Science fiction
.S83	Supernatural
.T55	Time
.U8	Utopias

COLLECTIONS OF AMERICAN LITERATURE [anthologies]

Special topics (Prose and verse), A-Z

PS509	.A85	Atomic weapons and disarmament
	.C59	Computers
	.D4	Death
	.F3	Fantasy
	.G5	Ghosts
	.I58	Interplanetary voyages
	.P6	Poe, Edgar Allan
	.S65	Space
	.T85	Twenty-first century
	.W57	Witchcraft

Poetry. By subject, A-Z

PS595	.A84	Atomic power
	.D42	Death
	.E93	Extinct animals
	.F36	Fantasy
	.H35	Halloween
	.I46	Imagination
	.I57	Interplanetary voyages
	.M96	Mysticism
	.S35	Science fiction
	.S77	Spiders

Drama. By subject, A-Z

PS627	.S39	Science fiction plays

Prose (General). Special forms and topics, A-Z

PS648	.C65	Computers
	.F3	Fantastic fiction
	.F87	Future life
	.G48	Ghost stories
	.H22	Halloween
	.H6	Horror tales
	.L53	Life on other planets
	.M25	Magic
	.M3	Mars (Planet)
	.M54	Monsters
	.N83	Nuclear warfare
	.S3	Science fiction
	.U85	Utopias
	.V35	Vampires
	.V66	Voodooism
	.W37	Werewolves
	.W5	Witchcraft
	.W58	Wolf children

CLASS PT (GERMANIC LITERATURES)

GERMAN LITERATURE

History. Special subjects

PT134	.D9	Dwarfs
PT148	.S3	Science
	.S8	Supernatural
	.U85	Utopias
	.V3	Vampires

History. Modern. 18th-19th centuries. Special subdivisions: 1789/1800-1830/50. Romanticism. Special topics, A-Z

PT363	.D6	Doppelgänger
	.G6	Gothic horror tales. Nachtstücke

History. Special forms. Poetry. Special topics, A-Z

PT509	.U54	Unicorns

History. Prose. Prose fiction. Special kinds, A-Z

    PT747   .F3   Fantastic fiction
                   .S34   Science fiction

Collections. Prose fiction. Special forms, A-Z

    PT1340   .F35   Fantastic fiction
                  .H6   Horror tales

AUSTRIAN LITERATURE

Collections. Other special, A-Z

    PT3826   .F2   Fantastic fiction

DUTCH LITERATURE

Collections. Prose. Prose fiction. Special, A-Z

    PT5532   .F35   Fantastic fiction
                  .S3   Science fiction

NORWEGIAN LITERATURE

Collections. Prose. Fiction. Special, A-Z

    PT8723   .S3   Science fiction

P-PZ LITERATURE TABLES

Grammar. Readers on special subjects, A-Z. Tables I-V, p. 3: 127/.2/.15/.15/none

                    .F35   Fantastic fiction

History and criticism. Prose. Fiction. History. Special topics, A-Z
Tables XX-XXI, p. 18: 107/12.6

                    .F27   Fantastic fiction
                    .G74   Grotesque
                    .S34   Science fiction
                    .S8   Supernatural

.U86 Utopias

Collections. Special topics, A-Z. Tables XX-XXI, p. 19: 136.5/14.52:

.F36 Fantasy
.S33 Science fiction

Individual authors or works. Criticism and interpretation. Treatment and knowledge of special subjects, A-Z. Table XXXI, p. 31: 42/92

.A4 Allegory
.D4 Devil
.F35 Fairy tales
.G7 Grotesque
.M96 Myth
.T5 Time

Criticism. Special. Other, A-Z. Tables XXXII-XXXIII, p. 34-36: 17/8

.A6 Allegory
.E9 Evil
.F33 Fairies
.I44 Immortality
.M34 Marvelous
.M47 Metamorphosis
.O25 Occultism
.T54 Time
.U76 Utopias

CLASS QA (MATHEMATICS)

Geometry.

QA699 Hyperspace. Popular Works. Fiction

CLASS TR (PHOTOGRAPHY)

Cinematography. Motion pictures. Special photographic processes

TR858 Trick cinematography [special effects]

CLASS U (MILITARY SCIENCE)

U310   War games. Kriegspiel
U313   Imaginary wars and battles (General)

CLASS V (NAVAL SCIENCE)

V253   Imaginary naval wars and battles

CLASS Z (LIBRARY SCIENCE AND BIBLIOGRAPHY)

Bookselling and publishing. Special kinds of business, A-Z

   Z286   .F3   Fantastic fiction. Science fiction

   United States. History. Biography. Including histories of individual firms

   Z473   .A68   Arkham House
              .D29   DAW Books, Inc.
              .N46   Newcastle Publishing Co.
              .R42   Reginald, R.

Libraries. Library science. The collections. The books. Special collections, A-Z

   Z688   .S32   Science fiction

Classification and notation. By subject or form, A-Z

   Z697   .F29   Fantastic fiction

Imaginary books and libraries

   Z1024

National bibliography. United States. American literature. Special topics, A-Z

   Z1231   .D55   Dime novels
              .F32   Fantastic literature

   Great Britain and Ireland. Literature (general). Special topics, A-Z

   Z2014   .H67   Horror tales

    .S33 Science fiction
    .U84 Utopias

Italy. Literature (general). Special topics, A-Z

 Z2354 .S33 Science fiction

Communication. Mass media. Special topics, A-Z

 Z5633 .S34 Science fiction

Subject bibliography. Fiction. Special topics, A-Z

 Z5917 .F3 Fantastic fiction
     .G45 Ghost stories
     .G66 Gothic revival
     .N83 Nuclear warfare
     .S36 Science fiction

Folklore. Special topics, A-Z

 Z5983 .F17 Fairy tales
     .V36 Vampires

Geography and travels. Maps. Cartography. Voyages and travels. Imaginary voyages

 Z6017 .A1 A-Z, General bibliography
     .A3-Z Special

Tables. Table I, p. 272-273

 (14)   .F34 Fantastic literature
     .H67 Horror tales
     .S33 Science fiction

INDEX TO CLASSIFICATION NUMBERS

Adventure films: PN1995.9.A3.
Alchemy in drama: PN6150.A42.
Alchemy in literature. History: English Elizabethan literature: PR429.A35
Allegory in literature. Criticism: American prose fiction: PS374.A45; English literature: PR149.A635; modern English literature: PR408.A4; P-PZ tables: XXXI: 42/92.A4, XXXII-XXXIII: 17/8.A6. Philosophy: PN56.A5.
Androids in art: NC825.A53.
Apocalypse in literature. Collections: General: PN6071.A78. Criticism: American literature: PS169.A66; American prose fiction: PS374.A65.
Arkham House. History: Z473.A68.
Arthurian legends and romances. Collections: PN6071.A84. Criticism: American prose fiction: PS374.A78; English literature: PR149.A79; English prose fiction: PR830.A76; modern English literature: PR408.A7. Italian literature: PQ4053.A7. Philosophy: PN57.A6.
Astrology in drama. Criticism: English 16th century drama: PR658.A8.
Astrology in literature. Criticism: English literature: PR149.A798. Wit and humor: PN6231.A73.
Astronautics in literature. Philosophy: PN56.A8.
Astronomy in literature. Criticism: English literature: PR149.A8. Theory: PN56.A82
Atlases of imaginary, literary, and mythological regions: G3122.
Atomic power in poetry. Collections: American poetry: PS595.A84.
Atomic weapons in literature. Collections: American literature: PS509.A85.
Automata [robots] in literature. Collections: PN6071.A94. Philosophy: PN56.A9.
Avalon in literature. Criticism: English 20th century fiction: PR888.A76.
Bibliography. Fairy tales: Z5983.F17. Fantastic literature: Z5917.F3; American fantastic fiction: Z1231.F32; Z tables: (14).F34. Ghost stories: Z5917.G45. Gothic revival: Z5917.G66. Horror tales:

British literature: Z2014.H67; Z tables: (14).H67. Imaginary voyages: Z6017. Nuclear warfare: Z5917.N83. Science fiction: Z5917.S36; Science fiction in mass media: Z5633.S34; British science fiction: Z2014.S33; Italian science fiction: Z2354.S33; Z tables: (14).S33. British utopias: Z2014.U84.
Book jackets: NC1882.7.
Bookselling and publishing. Fantastic literature and science fiction: Z286.F3.
Classification. Fantastic literature: Z697.F29.
Computers in literature. Collections: American literature: PS509.C59; American prose: PS648.C65.
Cosmogony in literature. Collections: PN6071.C76.
Cosmology in literature. Philosophy: PN56.C68.
Curiosities and wonders in literature. Wit and humor: PN6231.C85.
Cybernetics in literature. Criticism: American prose fiction: PS374.C9.
DAW Books, Inc. History: Z473.D29.
Death and immortality in poetry. Collections: PN6110.D4; American poetry: PS595.D42.
Death in drama. Criticism: English 16th century drama: PR658.D4.
Death in literature. Collections: PN6071.D4; American literature: PS509.D4. Criticism: English Elizabethan literature: PR429.D418; English prose fiction: PR830.D37; French literature: PQ145.1.D33. Wit and humor: PN6231.D35.
Devil in literature. Collections: PN6071.D4. Criticism: PN57.D4; American literature: PS169.D47; English literature: PR149.D47; P-PZ table XXXI: 42/92.D4.
Dime novels. Bibliography: United States: Z1231.D55. Criticism: American prose fiction: PS374.D5.
Doppelgänger in literature. Criticism: German Romantic literature: PT363.D6.
Dreams in literature. Collections: English literature: PR1111.D7.
Dreams in poetry. Criticism: English literature: PR508.D8.
Dwarfs in literature. Criticism: German literature: PT134.D9.
Dystopias. Criticism: American prose fiction: PS374.D96; English prose fiction: PR830.D96; English 20th century fiction: PR888.D96.
End of the world in literature. Collections: PN6071.E5. Criticism: American literature: PS169.E53. Philosophy: PN56.E63.
Everyman dramas. Collections: PN6120.E9.
Evil in literature. Criticism: P-PZ tables XXXII-XXXIII: 17/8.E9.
Evolution in literature. Criticism: English prose fiction: PR830.E93.
Extinct animals in poetry. Collections: American poetry: PS595.E93.
Extrasensory perception in literature. Collections: English prose: PR1309.E85.
Fairies in poetry. Collections: PN6110.F3; English literature: PR1195.F34, PR1195.F343. Criticism: English literature: PR508.F34.

Fairy tales. Fairies in literature. Bibliography: Z5983.F17. Collections: PN6071.F15; English prose: PR1309.F26. Criticism: PN3435; English literature: PR149.F3; English prose fiction: PR830.F27; French prose fiction: PQ637.F27; P-PZ table XXXI: 42/92.F35; tables XXXII-XXXIII: 17/8.F33. Wit and humor: PN6231.F283.
Fall of man in literature. Collections: English literature: PR1111.F27. Criticism: American prose fiction: PS374.F26. Philosophy: PN56.F29.
Fantastic art: N8217.F28, ND1460.F35, NX650.F36.
Fantastic fiction.
    Bibliography. General: Z5917.F3; Z tables: (14).F34. United States: Z1231.F32.
    Bookselling: Z286.F3.
    Classification and notation: Z697.F29.
    Collections. General: PN6071.F25. Fiction: PN6120.95.F25. American literature: PS509.F3; American prose: PS648.F3. Austrian literature: PT3826.F2. Canadian literature: PR9194.52.F36; Canadian prose fiction: PR9197.35.F35. Chinese literature: PL2629.F35. Dutch prose fiction: PT5532.F35. English prose: PR1309.F3. French literature: PQ1110.F3; French prose fiction: PQ1276.F3. German prose fiction: PT1340.F35. Italian prose: PQ4249.6.F34. P-PZ tables: XX-XXI: 136.5/14.52.F36.
    Criticism. General: PN3435. American 20th century literature: PS228.F35; American prose fiction: PS374.F27. Argentinian prose fiction: PQ6607.F27. English modern literature: PR409.F34; English 19th century literature: PR468.F35; English 20th century prose: PR478.F35; English prose: PR830.F3; English 19th century prose: PR868.F3; English 20th century prose: PR888.F3. French literature: PQ145.1.F32; French prose fiction: PQ637.F3. German prose: PT747.F3. Italian prose: PQ4181.F36. Japanese literature: PL721.F27. Mexican prose fiction: PQ7207.F27. Spanish prose fiction: PQ6256.F35. P-PZ tables XX-XXI: 107/12.6.F27.
    Grammar—Readers. P-PZ tables I-V: 127/.2/.15/.15/none.F35.
    Philosophy and theory: PN56.F34.
    Technique: PN3377.5.F34.
Fantastic films: PN1995.9.F36.
Fantastic poetry. Collections: PN6110.F33; American poetry: PS595.F36; English poetry: PR1195.F36. Criticism: Russian byliny: PG3104.2.F3.
Fantastic television programs: PN1992.8.F35.
Fantasy games: GV1469.6-.62.
Fantasy in mass media: P96.F36. United States: P96.F362.U66+
Fate and fatalism in literature. Collections: PN6071.F28. Criticism: English prose fiction: PR830.F35.
Faust dramas. Collections: PN6120.F33.

Faust in literature. Collections: PN6071.F33. Philosophy: PN57.F3.
Flying Dutchman in literature. Philosophy: PN56.F6.
Folklore in literature. Criticism: American literature: PS169.F64.
Frankenstein films: PN1995.9.F8.
Future in literature. Criticism: American prose fiction: PS374.F86.
Future life in literature. Collections: PN6071.F86.
Futurism in literature. Philosophy: PN56.F8.
Games, Fantasy: GV1202.F35.
Geographical myths in mass media: P96.G46.
Geometry in fiction: QA699.
Ghost plays. Collections: PN6120.G45.
Ghost poetry. Collections: PN6110.G52; English poetry: PR1195.G47.
Ghost stories.
    Bibliography: Z5917.G45.
    Collections. General: PN6071.G45. Fiction: PN6120.95.G45. American literature: PS509.G5; American prose: PS648.G48. Chinese literature: PL2629.G5. English literature: PR1111.G48; English prose: PR1309.G5.
    Criticism. Chinese literature: PL2419.G5. English modern literature: PR409.G56; English prose fiction: PR830.G45.
    Wit and humor: PN6231.G45.
Ghouls and ogres in literature. Wit and humor: PN6231.G47.
Giants in poetry. Collections: PN6110.G52.
Godzilla films: PN1995.5.G63.
Golem in literature. Collections: PN6071.G6. Philosophy: PN57.G56.
Good and evil in literature. Criticism: American literature: PS169.G66.
Gothic literature. Bibliography: Z5917.G66. Collections: English Gothic revival: PR1111.G67. Criticism: American prose fiction—Gothic revival: PS374.G68; English modern literature: PR408.G68; English 18th century literature: PR448.G6; English prose fiction: PR830.T3; German Romantic literature: PT363.G6.
Gravity in literature. Wit and humor: PN6231.G84.
Grotesque in art: N8217.G8.
Grotesque in drama: PN1650.G7.
Grotesque in literature. Collections: English literature: PR1111.G7. Criticism: English modern literature: PR409.G7; English Elizabethan literature: PR429.G76; English prose fiction: PR830.G7; P-PZ tables XX-XXI: 107/12.6.G74; table XXXI: 42/92.G7. Philosophy: PN56.G7.
Halloween in literature. Collections: American prose: PS648.H22.
Halloween in poetry. Collections: American poetry: PS595.H35.
Heaven in poetry. Collections: PN6110.H17.
Heroes in drama. Criticism: English 16th century drama: PR658.H42.
Heroes in literature. Collections; PN6071.H4. Criticism: English modern literature: PR409.H45; English 18th century fiction: PR858.H4.

Heroes in mass media: P96.H46.
Heaven in poetry. Collections: PN6110.H17.
Horror films: PN1995.9.H6.
Horror in art: N8217.H68; NC968.5.H6.
Horror in mass media: P96.H65.
Horror tales.
    Bibliography: British literature: Z2014.H67; Z tables: (14).H67.
    Collections. General: PN6071.H727. Fiction: PN6120.95.H727. American prose: PS648.H6. English prose: PR1309.H6. German prose: PT1340.H6.
    Communication and mass media: P96.H65.
    Criticism. General: PN3435. American prose fiction: PS374.H67. English prose fiction: PR830.T3. Russian literature: PG3098.H67.
    Illustration: N8217.H68, NC968.5.H6.
    Philosophy and theory: PN56.H6.
    Technique: PN3377.5.H67.
Hyperspace in fiction: QA699.
Illustration: NC825, NC961.7. Periodical illustration: NC968.5.
Imaginary books and libraries: Z1024.
Imaginary wars and battles: U313. Naval wars: V253.
Imagination in poetry. Collections: American poetry: PS595.I46.
Immortality in literature. Criticism: P-PZ tables XXXII-XXXIII: 17/8.I44.
Incubi in literature. Criticism: English literature: PR149.I58.
Interplanetary voyages—see: Voyages, Interplanetary.
Jewish legends and tales in literature. Collections: PN6071.J5.
Labyrinths in literature. Criticism: English 20th century literature: PR479.L35.
Lazarus in literature. Collections: PN6071.L35.
Libraries—special collections of science fiction: Z688.S32.
Life on other planets in literature. Collections: American prose: PS648.L53.
Magic in drama. Criticism: English 16th century drama: PR658.M27.
Magic in literature. Collections: PN6071.M155; American prose: PS648.M25.
Magic realism in literature. Philosophy: PN56.M24.
Man, Primitive, in literature. Collections: PN6071.M17.
Mars (Planet) in literature. Collections: American prose: PS648.M3.
Marvelous in literature. Collections: PN6071.M25. Criticism: P-PZ tables XXXII-XXXIII: 17/8.M34. Philosophy: PN56.M3.
Mesmerism in literature. Philosophy: PN56.M52.
Metamorphosis in literature. Criticism: P-PZ tables XXXII-XXXIII: 17/8.M47. Philosophy: PN56.M53.
Metamorphosis in poetry. Criticism: American literature: PS310.M37.
Millennialism in literature. Criticism: American prose fiction: PS374.M52.

Miracles in literature. Collections: PN6071.M54.
Monster films: PN1995.9.M6.
Monsters in art: NC825.M6.
Monsters in literature. Collections: American prose: PS648.M54; English literature: PR1111.M55. Communication: P96.M6. Criticism: English literature: PR149.M65. Philosophy: PN56.M55. Wit and humor: PN6231.M665.
Monsters in mass media: P96.M6.
Monsters in poetry. Collections: English literature: PR1195.M6.
Moon in literature. Collections: PN6071.M6.
Moon in poetry. Collections: PN6110.M6.
Mummies in literature. Collections: PN6071.M77.
Munchausen in literature. Philosophy: PN57.M77.
Mysticism in literature. Criticism: English literature tables (5).M9.
Mysticism in poetry. Collections: American poetry: PS595.M96
Myth in literature. Criticism: American prose fiction: PS374.M88; English 20th century literature: PR478.M96; French prose fiction: PQ637.M98; P-PZ table XXXI: 42/92.M96. Philosophy: PN56.M94.
Myth in poetry. Criticism: American poetry: PS310.M96; English poetry: PR508.M87, PR509.M92.
Mythology in films: PN1995.9.M97.
Mythology in literature. Criticism: American 20th century literature: PS228.M9; English literature: PR149.M95; English modern literature: PR409.M9. Philosophy: PN56.M95.
Mythology in poetry. Collections: PN6110.M8. Criticism: English literature: PR508.M9.
Newcastle Publishing Co. History: Z473.N46.
Nothingness in poetry. Criticism: American literature: PS310.N66.
Nuclear warfare in literature. Bibliography: Z5917.N83. Collections: American prose: PS648.N83. Philosophy: PN3352.N83.
Occultism in literature. Collections: PN6071.O22. Criticism: English modern literature: PR409.O28; English prose fiction: PR830.O33; P-PZ Tables XXXII-XXXIII: 17/8.O25. Philosophy: PN56.O33.
Otherworld in literature. Philosophy: PN56.O7.
Outer space in literature—see: Space and time in literature.
Outer space posters: NC1849.S63.
Pan (the deity) in literature: PN57.P25.
Parables in literature. Collections: PN6071.P27.
Paradise in literature. Criticism: English modern literature: PR409.P33.
Penny dreadfuls. Collections: English prose: PR1309.P45.
Periodical illustration: NC968.5.
Poe, Edgar Allan, in literature. Collections: American literature: PS509.P6.
Posters in art: NC1849.

Primitive society in literature. Criticism: English prose fiction: PR830.S65.
Prophecies in literature: Philosophy: PN56.P744.
Quests in literature. Criticism: American prose fiction: PS374.Q47.
Reginald, R. [Publisher]: Z473.R42.
Robinsonades. Criticism: PN3432.
Rockets in art: NC825.R6.
Satanism in literature. Collections: PN6071.S2.
Science fiction.
    Bibliography. General: Z5917.S36; Z tables: (14).S33. Great Britain: Z2014.S33; Italy: Z2354.S33. Communication: Z5633.S34.
    Collections. General: PN6071.S33. Fiction: PN6120.95.S33. American prose: PS648.S3. Australian prose fiction: PR9617.35.S33. Canadian prose fiction: PR9197.35.S33. Chinese fiction: PL2629.S34. Dutch prose fiction: PT5532.S3. English prose: PR1309.S3. French prose fiction: PQ1276.S35. Italian prose: PQ4249.6.S34. Norwegian prose fiction: PT8723.S3. Romanian prose: PC838.5.S3. Spanish prose: PQ6256.S34.
    Communication and mass media: P96.S34.
    Congresses: PN3433.2.
    Criticism. General: PN3433.5. American prose fiction: PS374.S35. Australian prose fiction: PR9612.6.S34. Canadian prose fiction: PR9192.6.S34. English prose fiction: PR830.S35; English Victorian fiction: PR878.S35. French prose fiction: PQ637.S34. German prose fiction: PT747.S34. Italian literature: PQ4053.S25; Italian prose: PQ4181.S35. Japanese literature: PL721.S3; Japanese prose fiction: PL740.65.S3. Russian 20th century literature: PG3025.S35; Russian prose fiction: PG3098.S5. P-PZ tables XXI-XXII: 107/12.6.S34; 176.5/17.35.S33.
    Encyclopedias and dictionaries: PN3433.4.
    Exhibitions: PN3433.3.
    History: PN3433.8.
    Library special collections: Z688.S32.
    Periodicals and societies: PN3433.
    Special topics: PN3433.6.
    Study and teaching: PN3433.7.
    Technique and authorship: PN3377.5.S3.
    Wit and humor. Collections: PN6231.S42.
Science fiction films: PN1995.9.S26.
Science fiction in art: NC825.S34, NC961.7.S34, NC968.5.S33, NC1882.7.S35, NX650.S3.
Science fiction in mass media: P96.S34.
Science fiction plays. Collections: American plays: PS627.S39.
Science fiction poetry. Collections: American poetry: PS595.S35.
Science in literature. Criticism: German literature: PT148.S3.

Science in poetry. Criticism: English poetry: PR509.S33.
Soul in poetry. Collections: English literature: PR1195.S65.
Space flight to the Moon in literature. Collections: PN6071.S58.
Space and time in literature. Criticism: American literature: PS228.O96; English 18th century literature: PR448.S69; French prose fiction: PQ637.S65. Philosophy: PN56.S667.
Space in poetry. Criticism: English poetry: PR508.S65.
Space travel in literature. Wit and humor: PN6231.S645.
Space vehicles in art: NC825.S58.
Special effects in films: TR858.
Spider [the magazine]: PN4878.5.S6.
Spiders in poetry. Collections: American poetry: PS595.S77.
Star trek films: PN1995.9.S694.
Stars in literature. Collections: PN6071.S67. Philosophy: PN56.S735.
Stars in poetry. Collections: PN6110.S75.
Sun in poetry. Collections: PN6110.S87.
Superman films: PN1995.9.S77.
Superman in literature: PN57.S94.
Superman in mass media: P96.S94.
Supernatural films: PN1995.9.S8.
Supernatural in literature.
- Collections. General: PN6071.S9. English literature: PR1111.S78. Criticism. American prose fiction: PS374.S83. English literature: PR147; English prose fiction: PR830.S85. German literature: PT148.S8. Japanese literature: PL721.S8. P-PZ tables XX-XXI: 107/12.6.S8.
- Philosophy and theory: PN56.S8.

Supernatural in poetry. Collections: PN6110.S9.
Superstition in literature. Wit and humor: PN6231.S88
Surrealism in literature. Criticism: English modern literature: PR408.S85. Philosophy: PN56.S87.
Surrealism in poetry. Collections: English poetry: PR1195.S87.
Surrealistic films: PN1995.9.S85.
Tales of terror—see: Gothic literature and Horror tales.
Tarzan films: PN1995.9.T3.
Tarzan in mass media: P96.T37.
Terror and wonder in poetry. Collections: PN6110.T5.
Time in drama: PN1650.T5.
Time in films: PN1995.9.T55.
Time in literature. Collections: PN6071.T5. Criticism: American literature: PS169.T5; American prose fiction: PS374.T55; English prose fiction: PR830.T5; P-PZ table XXXI: 42/92.T5; tables XXXII-XXXIII: 17/8.T54. Philosophy: PN56.T5. Wit and humor: PN6231.T64.
Twenty-first century in literature. Collections: American literature: PS509.T85.

Undine in literature: PN57.U5.
Unicorns in literature. Wit and humor: PN6231.U54.
Unicorns in poetry. Criticism: German literature: PT509.U54.
Utopias.
   Bibliography. Great Britain: Z2014.U84.
   Collections. General: HX810. American prose: PS648.U85.
   Criticism. General: PN3448.U7. American literature: PS169.U85; American 19th century literature: PS217.U8; American prose fiction: PS374.U8. Arabic literature: PJ7519.U85. English literature: PR149.U8; English prose: PR756.U86; English prose fiction: PR830.U7; English 20th century fiction: PR888.U7. German literature: PT148.U85. Russian prose fiction: PG3096.U94. P-PZ tables XX-XXI: 107/12.6.U86; tables XXXII-XXXIII: 17/8.U76.
   Philosophy and theory: PN56.U8.
Vampire films: PN1995.9.V3.
Vampires in literature. Bibliography: Z5983.V36. Collections: General: PN6071.V3; Fiction: PN6120.95.V3; American prose: PS648.V35; English prose: PR1309.V36. Criticism: English modern literature: PR409.V34; English 19th century literature: PR469.V35; German literature: PT148.V3. Philosophy: PN56.V3. Wit and humor: PN6231.V27.
Vampires in poetry. Collections: PN6110.V37.
Venus (the planet) in literature. Collections: English prose: PR1309.V4.
Voodooism in literature. Collections: American prose: PS648.V66.
Voyages, Imaginary. Bibliography: Z6017. Communication: P96.V68. Criticism: General: PN3432; English prose fiction: PR830.V6; French prose fiction: PQ637.V7. Philosophy: PN56.V59.
Voyages, Interplanetary, in literature. Collections: General: PN6071.I64; American literature: PS509.I58. Philosophy: PN56.V6.
Voyages, Interplanetary, in poetry. Collections: American poetry: PS595.I46.
Wandering Jew in literature: PN57.W3.
War games: U310.
Water sprites in literature. Philosophy: PN56.W37.
Werewolf films: PN1995.9.W38.
Werewolves in literature. Collections: American prose: PS648.W37.
Witchcraft in drama. Criticism: English 16th century drama: PR658.W58.
Witchcraft in literature. Collections: American literature: PS509.W57; American prose: PS648.W5; English prose: PR1309.W5. Criticism: American 19th century literature: PS217.W5; English modern literature: PR409.W57; English Elizabethan literature: PR429.W57. Philosophy: PN56.W49.
Wolf children in literature. Collections: American prose: PS648.W58.

III
AUTHOR MAIN ENTRIES AND LITERATURE NUMBERS

INTRODUCTION

Publication in 1978 of the second edition of the *Anglo-American Cataloging Rules*, and the subsequent adoption of these rules by the Library of Congress in 1980, has resulted in many changes in author main entries. In simplified form, AACR2 requires that catalogers use the writer's name as it actually appears on most of his or her books; authors using more than one name may either have their works centralized under the preeminent name, or split among several or all of his pseudonyms, if none truly predominates. Prior to AACR2, LC sometimes used common forms of names, but just as frequently adopted convoluted variations which bore little resemblance to the originals.

On the surface, AACR2 seems a logical simplification of previously abstruse cataloging rules, but problems have arisen in practice. The first changes were made in 1980, with a massive retrospective "sweep" through MARC (LC's giant data base), OCLC, and the other library data bases; a second large "sweep" was conducted in the summer of 1987 in OCLC, and such automated comparisons with LC's Name-Authority File will apparently be necessary for the indefinite future. Since LC does not normally recatalog books without reason, a great many authors who are dead or inactive, and whose status does not give them high literary visibility, continue to be listed in the *National Union Catalog* (and OCLC) under forms which are obsolete under AACR2; these names will be changed (if ever) only when a book by or about that author is newly cataloged by LC. Some libraries have arbitrarily assigned AACR2 forms to such writers when cataloging their books in OCLC; these names may differ slightly or radically from those already used by LC through 1980, from forms adopted after 1980, by LC or others, or from those which LC may ultimately choose, at some vague future date. Compounding the problem is the recent addition to OCLC of the national data bases of the British Library and the National Library of Canada, which often use forms of names which differ from those employed elsewhere. Thus, what began with the best of intentions as a "great simplification" has actually spawned greater inconsistencies than the system it replaced.

The Library of Congress must share some of the blame for the haphazard way in which the rules have been applied. On occasion, it will choose forms which clearly contradict AACR2 rules, or (more commonly) it will continue to use forms not precisely correct. For example, Douglas Menville, a film editor and critic, is cataloged by LC as Douglas Alver Menville, despite the fact that he never uses a middle name or initial; this form derives from his first published book, which was an exact reproduction of his thesis, middle name included. Although clearly erroneous under AACR2, it has not been changed by the Library of Congress. One can only presume that LC has made a conscious choice with certain middle-level writers to leave their entries as they existed prior to AACR2, on the theory that few users will care or even notice. This is unfortunate, since no one outside of the Library of Congress reviews these changes or is even aware of them until after they occur.

AACR2 also provides for the addition of dates to main entries to distinguish writers with the same names from each other; when dates cannot be determined, no further effort is made to separate them. The Library of Congress, however, sometimes adds such dates to previously-established main entries years after the original authority was first created, to resolve conflicts posed by newer main entries about which it has less information. Similarly, LC will occasionally split or merge main entries of authors with more than one pseudonym after doing precisely the opposite for extended periods of time. For example, Dean Koontz's main entry was split after the assumption of AACR2 into his component pseudonyms, his literature number being maintained under his real name (which he continued to use on some of his books). In the summer of 1987, after Koontz began to reissue his old books under his real name, LC changed its authority record, centralizing all of his names under "Koontz, Dean R. (Dean Ray), 1945- ". Thus, a library which had cataloged a book by "K.R. Dwyer" in the spring of 1987 would have used the main entry "Dwyer, K. R., 1945- ", with appropriate see also references; six months later, a different library cataloging the same book would have used "Koontz," with appropriate see references. In all likelihood, the original library will never notice the change.

Such wholesale retrospective alterations to LC's data base are unsettling and largely invisible, since few libraries in the 1980s (if any) are capable of catching such changes after the fact. OCLC does not include internal see references other than those generated (sometimes falsely) by its occasional "sweeps"; one must search LC's Name-Authority File to find them. Another example of this disturbing trend can be seen with "M.E. Chaber," a pseudonym of Kendell Foster Crossen. Crossen's books had been centralized under his real name prior to AACR2, but were split by LC in 1980 among his various pseudonyms. The effects of such splits are insidious; the 1987 OCLC data base "sweep," for example, did not affect books cataloged under "Crossen" which under the new rules should have been recataloged under his pennames, since "Crossen" itself remains a valid AACR2 heading—the system is too unsophisticated to identify errors of this type. Such discrepancies increase with each passing day; the 1987 OCLC "sweep" also erroneously matched several authors with see references generated for other writers in LC's Name-Authority File, and moved their records to inappropriate main entries.

These changes, although hidden from most librarians and patrons, have and will become more visible, with serious, long-term implications for data integrity, both at local and national levels. Searching OCLC well has become difficult even for the most sophisticated user, requiring considerable training and experience just to understand the vagaries of the system; this can only increase as the size of OCLC mushrooms (now increasing at the rate of 2.2 million records annually). Automated "sweeps," while useful in catching gross errors, are clearly only a stopgap. The Library of Congress must take the lead in reestablishing some commonsense standard for determining main entries, and must assist the library world in dealing with the tens of thousands of older author names that have yet to be "converted" to forms compatible with AACR2.

The main entries listed below have been checked in LC's Name-Authority File through the summer of 1987, and are correct as given; some will undoubtedly change before the second edition of this manual is published. Note that the Library of Congress, while it may add a date of birth (or even a *day* of birth, if necessary) to resolve name conflicts, does not normally add dates of death to an entry unless the author is long dead and his dates are well known, or unless his entire body of work is being reevaluated, as happened several years ago with Charles Beaumont; occasionally, such changes will occur serendipitously, often when an author dies just before his first or last book is published. More complete forms of an author's name are sometimes added in parentheses to differentiate similar names (*e.g.*, Compton, D. G. (David Guy), 1930-); the parenthesis or hyphen is considered terminating punctuation in such entries, no period being added. OCLC differs from AACR2 in placing titles such as "Sir" or "Mrs." after the author's given name, and I have followed such practice here.

In the previous edition of this cataloging manual, I tried to anticipate the adoption of AACR2 forms, with mixed results. Shortly after that book went to press, in 1984, LC's Name-Authority File was made available to OCLC users, and I have relied on it heavily in this book, despite the fact that it lacks many authors cataloged before 1980. I have dropped any forms which cannot be confirmed by LC's actual usage, reverting to pre-AACR2 forms where new versions are as yet unavailable.

AACR2 also issued new filing rules in 1978, changing to a system which closely resembles computer filing practices. Thus, blank spaces and most punctuations file ahead of anything else, numbers and symbols ahead of letters, each word being treated as a separate entity for filing purposes. This in turn has changed the way in which cutter numbers are assigned to both authors and titles in the literature schedules. Authors whose names were affected by the filing changes, and whose books were cataloged for the first time after 1980, have received literature numbers which put their names in proper alphabetical order under the new rules; but previously-established authors who had already received permanent literature numbers were not moved, and under LC's policy of leaving well enough alone, will not be. This has resulted in many discrepancies in the tables, most obviously with authors whose names begin with "Mc"; under the old rules, such names were filed as if spelled "Mac," subject cutters being assigned appropriately. Under AACR2, these names are now filed in strict order, and the subject cutters have changed to "C" for those authors who have been assigned numbers for the first time post-1980.

LC also decided that only one literature number would be assigned to each author, even if his main entries were split under more than one name; this may sometimes result in an author's literature number being out of sequence under the new rules, even when his entries *are* centralized (see, for example, the Authority record for Dennis Lynds, all of whose records are now centralized under his pseudonym, William Arden, but whose literature number continues to be generated from his real name; such anomalies are common under AACR2). Note that the alternate literature numbers assigned by LC between 1969-1980 to PZ3 and PZ4 classifications are not regarded by LC as permanent unless confirmed by later assignments. For a fuller explanation of LC's policies regarding the assignment of literature numbers for authors with split entries, see its *Cataloging Service Bulletin* No. 20 (Spring, 1983): 47-49.

In theory, the Library of Congress assigns literature numbers by language, nationality, and period, in that order. Under each period, authors are given numbers which put their names in strict alphabetical order (note again, however, that the change in filing rules in 1978 may affect the sequence of these names—and their classification numbers). American literature, for example, has two spans of numbers for the twentieth century, PS3500-3549 for authors active between 1900-1960, and PS3550-3576 for those active after 1960. The demarcations between these boundaries are often vague and ill-defined. PS3500 and PS3550 are reserved for anonymous works and for authors whose names consist only of punctuation or initialisms. PS3551-3576 corresponds, on a letter by number basis, to each letter of the alphabet, PS3551, for example, standing for all American writers active in the latter half of the twentieth century whose last names begin with "A."

Cutter numbers (from tables originally designed by Charles Cutter) complete the classification, providing a unique and unchangeable identification for each literary author (prior to 1900, authors may sometimes be given a span of numbers, particularly those with large bodies of work). The initial letter of the cutter corresponds to the second letter of the author's surname (or, in some foreign classifications, to the first changing element of the author's name). The number part of the classification is derived from the third letter of the author's name, and is expanded to whatever length may be necessary to create a unique number while maintaining proper alphabetical sequence. Very generally, the number "3" corresponds to the letter "a," "4" to "e," "5" to "i," "6" to "o," "7" to "r," "8" to "u," and "9" to "y"; these are not fixed, and may be adjusted to fit particular circumstances. For example, Edmund Cooper has the number PR6053.O5469; this falls between O53 (for Michael Cooney) and O55 (for Giles Cooper). Each digit of the number represents a further *sub*division, not some greater amount. This becomes more obvious when one looks closely at the tables. A more detailed explanation of the literature tables can be found at the end of this section.

The author's literature number is immutable once assigned; a second cutter is used to create a similar number for each of the writer's literary works. Hence, Robert A. Heinlein's novel, *Friday*, could be classed in PS3515.E288F7 1987, for a printing issued in 1987. All of an author's fiction, drama, poetry, and other literary productions are assigned numbers which place them in strict alphabetical sequence, with some exceptions (explained at the end of this section); books on other subjects, including literary subjects, receive classification numbers appropriate to those subjects, and are not classed as literature.

The literature numbers provided below are those actually developed by LC, as permanent or alternate numbers, through mid-1987, unless the latter are clearly erroneous (perhaps a half dozen); the alternate numbers may eventually change (when confirmed) if the author's main entry has changed, or if some other conflict has since developed, but most will remain the same. Where no literature number exists, or where only juvenile numbers (PZ7+) have been assigned, I use the word "none." LC does not normally catalog mass market paperback fiction; thus, only writers with cloth or trade paperback editions to their credit usually have classification numbers. I also include here (in parentheses) bibliography numbers from the "Z" schedule, for the few authors who have them. The "Z" schedule was the first to be developed at LC, in the late 1890s, and it remains the most primitive, in both style and function. Essentially, it puts authors in alphabetical order by main entry, assigning whole and subdivided numbers in a span from Z8000-8999. Many libraries have abandoned these numbers, preferring to class bibliographies with other nonfiction books about the author. Note that writers may have more than one literature number, if they have written original books in more than one language (Vladimir Nabokov wrote in Russian, French, and English, and thus has three numbers). There are also several authors who have accidentally been assigned more than one number by LC, without priority; I list both numbers until the conflict is resolved.

SCIENCE FICTION AUTHORS AND LITERATURE NUMBERS

Aaron, Chester.	none
Ab Hugh, Davydd.	none
Abbey, Edward, 1927-	PS3551.B2
Abbey, Lynn.	PS3551.B23
Abbott, Edwin Abbott, 1838-1926.	none
Abbott, Keith, 1944-	PS3551.B26
Abdullah, Achmed, 1881-1945.	PS3501.B3
Abe, Kobo, 1924-	PL845.B4
Abel, R. Cox.	none
Ableman, Paul.	PR6051.B5
About, Edmond, 1828-1885.	PQ2151
Abramov, Aleksandr Ivanovich, fl. 1967-	PG3242.2.A27
Abramov, Sergei, 1944-	none
Abrams, R. Vaughn, 1949-	PS3551.B67
Abrashkin, Raymond, 1911-1960.	none
Ackerman, Forrest J.	none
Ackroyd, Peter.	PR6051.C64
Adair, Gilbert.	PR6051.D287
Adams, Douglas, 1952-	PR6051.D3352
Adams, Hunter.	none
Adams, Ian.	PR9199.3.A25
Adams, John—see: Glasby, John.	
Adams, Richard, 1920-	PR6051.D345
Adams, Robert, 1933-	PS3551.D395
Adams, Terry A.	none
Adkins, Patrick H.	none
Adlard, Mark.	PR6051.D55
Adleman, Robert H., 1919-	PS3551.D57
Adler, Allen A., 1916-	none
Adler, Paul.	none
Adrian, Jack.	none
Affabee, Eric.	none
Aguilera Malta, Demetrio, 1909-	PQ8219.A36
Ahern, Jerry.	none
Ahern, S. A.	none
Aickman, Robert.	PR6051.I3
Aiken, Joan, 1924-	PR6051.I35
Aiken, John, 1913-	PR6051.I36
Aikin, Jim.	none
Ainsworth, William Harrison, 1805-1882.	PR4002-4003 [Z8020.2]
Airey, Jean.	PS3551.I57
Akers, Alan Burt—see: Bulmer, Kenneth, 1921-	
Akutagawa, Ryunosuke, 1892-1927.	PL801.K8

Alban, Antony.	[Z8020.45] none
Albano, Peter.	none
Alcock, Vivien.	none
Aldiss, Brian Wilson, 1925-	PR6051.L3 [Z8025.45]
Alexander, C. M.	none
Alexander, David M.	PS3551.L349
Alexander, Karl.	PS3551.L3569
Alexander, Lloyd.	PS3501.L435
Alexander, Thea.	none
Alfvén, Hannes, 1908-	PT9876.L46
Allaby, Michael.	none
Allen, Dick, 1939-	PS3551.L3922
Allen, Grant, 1848-1899.	PR4004.A2
Allen, Roger MacBride.	none
Allhoff, Fred.	PS3501.L55895
Alper, Gerald A.	none
Alter, Robert Edmond.	PS3551.L767
Altman, Thomas.	PS3551.L795
Al'tov, G (Genrikh)	PG3478.L73
Alverson, Charles E.	PS3551.L86
Amado, Jorge, 1912-	PQ9697.A647
Ames, Mildred.	none
Amis, Kingsley.	PR6001.M6 [Z8032.52]
Amosov, Nikolai Mikhailovich.	PG3478.M6
Anderson, Chester, 1932-	PS3551.N358
Anderson, Colin.	PR6051.N39
Anderson, Karen.	none
Anderson, Margaret Jean, 1931-	none
Anderson, Michael Falconer.	PR6051.N396
Anderson, Olof W.	PS3501.N284
Anderson, Paul Dale.	PS3551.N3777
Anderson, Poul, 1926-	PS3551.N378 [Z8035.55]
Anderson, William C.	PS3551.N4
Andersson, C. Dean.	none
Andreissen, David.	PS3551.N4135
Andrews, Allen.	PR6051.N457
Andrews, Lewis M.	none
Angelo, Ivan.	PQ9698.1.N474
Anstey, F., 1856-1934.	PR4728.G5
Anthony, Piers.	PS3551.N73
Antill, Keith.	PR9619.3.A67
Anvic, Frank—see: Sherman, Jory.	

Anvil, Christopher.	PS3551.N9
Appel, Allen.	PS3551.P55
Appel, Benjamin, 1907-	none
Appleton, Victor, II.	none
Appleton, Victor, pseud.	none
Arch, E. L.—see: Payes, Rachel Cosgrove.	
Arden, William, 1924-	PS3562.Y44
Ariss, Bruce.	none
Arkham, Candice.	PS3551.R437
Arlen, Michael, 1895-1956.	PR6001.R7
Armstrong, F. W.	none
Armstrong, Michael.	none
Arnason, Eleanor.	none
Arnold, Edwin Lester Linden, d. 1935.	PR6001.R775
Arrow, William.	none
Arscott, David.	PR9199.3.A7
Arthur, David Stuart.	PS3551.R74
Ashby, Richard.	none
Ashe, Geoffrey.	PR6051.S457
Ashe, Rosalind.	PR6051.S47
Asher, Marty.	PS3551.S375
Ashley, Steven.	none
Ashton, Francis Leslie, 1904-	PR6051.S5
Asimov, Isaac, 1920-	PS3551.S5
	[Z8045.59]
Asimov, Janet.	PS3560.E6
Asimow, Morris.	none
Asnin, Scott.	none
Asprin, Robert.	PS3551.S6
Asquith, Cynthia, Lady, 1887-1960.	PR6001.S68
Asturias, Miguel Angel.	PQ7499.A75
	[Z8045.8]
Atkins, Meg Elizabeth.	PR6051.T5
Attanasio, A. A.	PS3551.T74
Attwood, Tony.	none
Atwood, Margaret Eleanor, 1939-	PR9199.3.A8
Aubrey, Frank.	PR6001.U27
Auel, Jean M.	PS3551.U36
Augustus, Albert—see: Nuetzel, Charles.	
Aultman, Mark.	PS3551.U5
Auster, Paul, 1947-	PS3551.U77
Austin, Richard.	PR6051.U84
Avallone, Michael.	PS3551.V3
Avery, Richard—see: Cooper, Edmund, 1926-	
Avi, 1937-	none
Axler, James.	none

Aycock, Dale.	none
Aymé, Marcel, 1902-1967.	PQ2601.Y5
Bach, Richard.	PS3552.A255
Bachman, Richard.	PS3561.I483
Bacon, Walter.	PR6052.A313
Baehr, Patricia Goehner.	none
Baen, James Patrick—see: Baen, Jim.	
Baen, Jim.	none
Bagnall, R. D.	none
Bailey, Dennis R.	none
Bailey, Gerald Earl.	PS3552.A367
Bailey, John, 1944-	PR6052.A3187
Bailey, Robin W.	none
Bain, F. W. (Francis William), 1863-1940.	PR6003.A4
Bair, Patrick.	PR6052.A32
Baker, Betty.	none
Baker, Denys Val—see: Val Baker, Denys, 1917-	
Baker, Frank, 1908-	PR6003.A453
Baker, Jane.	none
Baker, Pip.	none
Baker, Scott.	PS3552.A4345
Baker, Sharon.	none
Baker, William Howard.	PR6052.A37
Balchin, Nigel, 1908-1970.	PR6003.A52
Baldwin, Bill.	none
Baldwin, Meri.	none
Ball, Brian N.	PR6052.A42
Ballard, J. G., 1930-	PR6052.A46 [Z8068.94]
Ballinger, W. A.—see: Baker, William Howard.	
Ballou, Arthur W.	none
Balmer, Edwin, 1883-	none
Balzac, Honoré de, 1799-1850.	PQ2157-2185 [Z8069.2]
Banerji, Sara, 1932-	PR6052.A483
Bangs, John Kendrick, 1862-1922.	PS1064.B3
Banister, Manly Miles, 1914-	none
Banks, Iain.	PR6052.A485
Banks, Lynne Reid.	none
Banks, Michael.	none
Bannister, Jo.	PR6052.A497
Bannon, Mark.	PR6063.U39
Barbet, Pierre.	none
Barclay, Alan.	none
Barjavel, René, 1911-	PQ2603.A435
Barker, Clive, 1952-	PR6052.A6475

Barker, D. A.	none
Barker, Muhammad Abd-al-Rahman.	none
Barker, Nicholas.	PR6052.A64875
Barker, Thomas W.	none
Barker, Wade.	none
Barnes, Arthur K.	none
Barnes, John, 1957-	PS3552.A677
Barnes, Rory.	PR9619.3.B334
Barnes, Steven.	none
Barnwell, William.	none
Barr, Donald.	PS3552.A7317
Barr, Tyrone C.	none
Barren, Charles.	none
Barrett, Geoffrey John.	PR6052.A717
Barrett, Michael Dennis.	none
Barrett, Neal.	PS3552.A7362
Barrett, Nicholas.	PR6052.A722
Barrett, William Edmund, 1900-	PS3503.A62873
Barrie, Monica.	none
Barringer, Leslie.	PR6003.A778
Barry, Jonathan—see: Strieber, Whitley.	
Barth, John.	PS3552.A75 [Z8076.7]
Bartholomew, Barbara, 1941-	PS3552.A7637
Barton, Erle—Fanthorpe, R. Lionel.	
Barton, James.	none
Barton, Lee—see: Fanthorpe, R. Lionel.	
Barton, S. W.	none
Barton, William.	none
Bartram, George, 1931-	PS3553.A4335
Barzman, Ben.	none
Bass, T. J.	none
Batchelor, John Calvin.	PS3552.A8268
Bateman, Robert.	none
Bates, Brian.	PR6052.A777
Bates, Harry.	none
Bauer, Steven.	PS3552.A8364
Baughman, Grace A.	PS3552.A837
Baum, L. Frank (Lyman Frank), 1856-1919.	PS3503.A923 [Z8080]
Baxter, John, 1939-	PR9619.3.B36
Baxter, Lorna.	PR6052.A848
Bayley, Barrington J.	PS3552.A87
Baylus, Robert F.	none
Bayly, Joseph.	PS3552.A88
Bayne, Neil F.	none

Beach, Lynn.	none
Beagle, Peter S.	PS3552.E13
Beale, Charles Willing, 1845-1932.	PS3503.E1173
Beamer, Charles.	PS3552.E15
Bear, David.	PS3552.E155
Bear, Greg, 1951-	PS3552.E157
Beasley, Conger.	PS3552.E175
Beatty, Jerome.	none
Beaumont, Charles, 1929-1967.	PS3552.E2316 [Z8085.5]
Bechdolt, Jack, 1884-	none
Beck, L. Adams (Lily Adams), d. 1931.	PS3503.E18
Beckford, William, 1760-1844.	PR4091-4092 [Z8086.4]
Bedford-Jones, H. (Henry), 1887-1949.	none
Beeching, Jack.	PR6003.E295
Beere, Peter.	none
Belanger, Sharlene.	none
Belden, David.	none
Belden, Wilanne Schneider.	none
Beliaev, A. (Aleksandr), 1884-1942.	PG3476.B42
Bell, Clare.	none
Bell, Eric Temple, 1883-1960.	PR6003.E4255
Bell, Gordon B. (Gordon Bennett)	PS3552.E513
Bell, Neil, 1887-1964.	PR6037.O843
Bell, Thornton—see: Fanthorpe, R. Lionel.	
Bellairs, John.	PS3552.E53
Bellamy, Edward, 1850-1898.	PS1086-1087 [Z8086.93]
Bellamy, Francis Rufus, 1886-	none
Belloc, Hilaire, 1870-1953.	PR6003.E45 [Z8087.7]
Bemmann, Hans, 1922-	none
Benét, Stephen Vincent, 1898-1943.	PS3503.E5325
Benford, Gregory, 1941-	PS3552.E542
Benjamin, Jacob.	none
Bennet, Robert Ames, 1870-	PS3503.E54547
Bennett, Gary L.	PS3552.E54584
Bennett, Gertrude Barrows, 1884-	PS3503.E5472
Bennett, Marcia J.	none
Bennett, Margot, 1903-	PR6003.E646
Benni, Stefano, 1947-	PQ4862.E565
Benoist, Elizabeth S.	PS3552.E5476
Benoit, Hendra.	none
Benoît, Pierre, 1886-1962.	PQ2603.E583
Bensen, D. R. (Donald R.), 1927-	PS3552.E54765

Benson, Arthur Christopher, 1862-1925.	PR4099.B5
Benson, E. F. (Edward Frederic), 1867-1940.	PR6003.E66
Benson, Nella.	none
Benson, Robert Hugh, 1871-1914.	PR6003.E7
Benson, Stella, 1892-1933.	PR6003.E72
Bent, Jorj.	none
Benting, Michael.	none
Berdnyk, Oleksandr Pavlovych.	PG3986.E8
Beresford, Elisabeth.	PR6052.E562
Beresford, John Davys, 1873-1947.	PR6003.E73
Beresford, Leslie.	none
Bergamini, David, 1928-	none
Berger, Thomas, 1924-	PS3552.E719
Bergin, Paul A.	none
Berk, Howard.	PS3552.E7195
Berlyn, Michael.	none
Berman, Mitch, 1956-	PS3552.E7252
Bernanos, Michael.	PQ2662.E686
Bernard, Rafe.	none
Berry, Adrian.	none
Berry, Bryan.	none
Berry, D. Bruce.	none
Berry, James R.	none
Berry, Stephen Ames.	none
Bertin, Jack.	none
Besant, Walter, Sir, 1836-1901.	PR4106
Besaw, Victor.	none
Bester, Alfred.	PS3552.E796 [Z8092.17]
Bethancourt, T. Ernesto.	none
Beverley, Barrington.	none
Bevis, H. U. (Herbert Urlin), 1903-	none
Beyer, William Gray.	none
Beynon, John—see: Wyndham, John, 1903-1969.	
Bickerton, Derek.	PR6052.I23
Bickham, Jack M.	PS3552.I3
Bidmead, Christopher H.	none
Biemiller, Carl L.	none
Bierce, Ambrose, 1842-1914?	PS1097 [Z8094.3]
Biggle, Lloyd, 1923-	PS3552.I43
Bilenkin, Dmitrii.	PG3479.4.I4
Bill, Alfred Hoyt, 1879-	PS3503.I553
Billias, Stephen.	none
Binder, Eando.	none
Binder, Otto O. (Otto Oscar), 1911-	none

Bingeman, Alison.	none
Bingham, Carson—see: Cassiday, Bruce.	
Bioy Casares, Adolfo.	PQ7797.B535
Birkin, Charles.	none
Bischoff, David.	PS3552.I759
Bischoff, Heather Woodard.	none
Bishop, George, 1924-	PS3552.I7598
Bishop, Michael.	PS3552.I772
Bishop, W. M.	none
Bishop, Zealia Brown.	PS3503.I8124
Bisson, Terry.	PS3552.I7736
Bixby, E. Rew.	none
Bixby, Jerome.	none
Black, Campbell.	PR6052.L25
Black, Ian Stuart, 1915-	PR6052.L3
Blackburn, John, 1923-	PR6052.L34
Blackden, Paul.	none
Blackford, Russell.	none
Blackstock, Charity.	PR6052.L3417
Blackwood, Algernon, 1869-1951.	PR6003.L3 [Z8102.23]
Blake, William Dorsey.	none
Blakeney, Jay D.—see: Chester, Deborah.	
Blamires, Harry.	PS3503.L39
Bland, Jay.	none
Blatty, William Peter.	PS3552.L392
Blavatsky, H. P. (Helena Petrovna), 1831-1891.	none
Blaylock, James P., 1950-	PS3552.L3966
Blayn, Hugo—see: Fearn, John Russell, 1908-1960.	
Blayre, Christopher—see: Heron-Allen, Edward, 1861-1943.	
Blish, James.	PS3503.L64
Bloch, Robert, 1917-	PS3503.L718
Block, Thomas.	PS3552.L634
Bloom, Harold.	PS3552.L6392
Blum, Ralph, 1932-	PS3552.L84
Blum, Robert S.	none
Blumlein, Michael.	PS3552.L855
Bodelsen, Anders, 1937-	PT8176.12.O34
Bogdanov, A. (Aleksandr), 1873-1928.	PG3467.M29
Bogner, Norman, 1935-	PS3552.O45
Boisgilbert, Edmund—see: Donnelly, Ignatius, 1831-1901.	
Bok, Hannes, 1914-1964.	PS3503.O333
Boland, John, 1913-	PR6052.O36
Bonanno, Margaret Wander.	PS3552.O5925
Bond, J. Harvey—see: Winterbotham, Russell Robert, 1904-	
Bond, Nancy.	none

Bond, Nelson Slade, 1908-	PS3503.O4286
Bone, Jesse Franklin, 1916-	PS3552.O598
Bonham, Frank.	PS3503.O4315
Bontly, Thomas J.	PS3552.O643
Boorman, John, 1933-	none
Boothby, Guy Newell, 1867-1905.	PR4149.B957
Bosse, Malcolm J. (Malcolm Joseph), 1934-	PS3552.O77
Bosshardt, Robert.	none
Boucher, Anthony, 1911-1968.	PS3545.H6172
Boulle, Pierre, 1912-	PQ2603.O754
Boult, S. Kye—see: Cochrane, William E.	
Bounds, Sydney J.	none
Bova, Ben, 1932-	PS3552.O84
Bowen, John, 1924-	PR6052.O85
Bowen, Marjorie, pseud.	PR6003.O676
Bowen, Robert Sydney, 1900-	none
Bowers, R. L.—see: Glasby, John.	
Bowes, Richard.	none
Bowker, Richard.	PS3552.O8739
Boyce, Chris.	PR6052.O917
Boyd, John, 1919-	PS3570.P35
Boye, Karin, 1900-1941.	PT9875.B69
Boyer, Elizabeth.	PS3552.O892
Boyett, Steven R.	none
Brackett, Leigh.	PS3503.R154
Bradbury, Edward P.—see: Moorcock, Michael, 1939-	
Bradbury, Ray, 1920-	PS3503.R167 [Z8113.3]
Bradford, Robert.	none
Bradley, Marion Zimmer.	PS3552.R228
Bradshaw, Gillian, 1956-	PS3552.R235
Bradshaw, William Richard, 1851-1927.	PS3503.R2265
Brady, Michael.	PS3552.R2436
Bramah, Ernest, 1869?-1942.	PR6037.M425
Brand, Christianna, 1907-	PR6023.E96
Brand, Kurt.	none
Brand, Larry.	none
Brandão, Ignácio de Loyola, 1936-	PQ9698.12.R293
Brandel, Marc, 1919-	PS3503.R25784
Brandner, Gary.	PS3552.R313
Branley, Franklyn Mansfield, 1915-	none
Brantenberg, Gerd, 1941-	PT8951.12.R34
Brautigan, Richard.	PS3503.R2736
Breggin, Peter Roger, 1936-	PS3552.R365
Brennan, J. H.	PR6052.R412
Brennan, Jan—see: Brennan, J. H.	

Brennan, Joseph Payne, 1918-	PS3503.R455
Brennan, Noel-Anne.	none
Brennert, Alan.	none
Brent, Jeremy.	none
Bretnor, Reginald.	PS3552.R395 [Z8118.44]
Brett, Leo—see: Fanthorpe, R. Lionel.	
Brice, Martin Hubert, 1935-	none
Bridges, Thomas Charles, 1868-	none
Briggs, Raymond.	PR6052.R4443
Brightfield, Richard.	none
Brin, David.	PS3552.R4825
Brindel, June Rachuy.	PS3552.R483
Britain, Dan—see: Pendleton, Don.	
Brittain, Bill.	none
Brockley, Fenton—see: Rowland, Donald S.	
Broderick, Damien.	PR9619.3.B698
Brontë, Charlotte, 1816-1855.	PR4165-4169
Bronte, Louisa—see: Roberts, Janet Louise, 1925-1982.	
Brooke-Rose, Christine, 1923-	PR6003.R412
Brookes, Owen.	PR6052.R5815
Brooks, Terry.	PS3552.R6596
Brooks, Walter R., 1886-1958.	none
Brooks-Janowiak, Jean.	none
Brophy, Brigid, 1929-	PR6052.R583
Brosnan, John.	none
Broster, Dorothy Kathleen.	PR6003.R433
Brown, Carter, 1923-	PR6052.R5893
Brown, Dennis Phillip.	none
Brown, Fredric, 1906-1972.	PS3503.R8135 [Z8123.593]
Brown, Harrison, 1917-1986.	none
Brown, James Cooke, 1921-	none
Brown, Jerry Earl.	none
Brown, Mary, 1929-	PR6052.R6143
Brown, Robin.	PR6052.R616
Brown, Rosel George.	PS3503.R828437
Brown, Slater, 1896-	none
Browne, C. J.	none
Browne, Gerald A.	PS3552.R746
Browne, Howard, 1908-	PS3503.R8436
Browne, Robert—see: Karlins, Marvin.	
Broxon, Mildred Downey.	PS3552.R7913
Bruce, Muriel.	PR9199.3.B738
Brunner, John, 1934-	PR6052.R8
Brush, Karen A.	none

Brust, Steven, 1955-	PS3552.R84
Bryan, Christopher, 1935-	PR6052.R88
Bryant, Dorothy, 1930-	PS3552.R878
Bryant, Edward, 1945-	PS3552.R879
Bryant, Peter.	PR6057.E54
Bryher, 1894-	PR6003.R98
Bucar, Cary A.	none
Buchan, John, 1875-1940.	PR6003.U13
Buchanan, Marie.	PR6054.U36
Buckley, William F. (William Frank), 1925-	PS3552.U344
Budrys, Algis, 1931-	PS3552.U348 [Z8129.67]
Buell, John.	PS3552.U373
Bujold, Lois McMaster.	none
Bulgakov, Mikhail Afanas'evich, 1891-1940.	PG3476.B78 [Z8130.45]
Bull, Emma.	none
Bulmer, H. K.—see: Bulmer, Kenneth, 1921-	
Bulmer, Kenneth, 1921-	none
Bulychev, K. (Kirill)	PG3479.4.U79
Bunch, Chris.	PS3552.U466
Bunch, David R.	none
Bunting, Eve, 1928-	none
Burdekin, Katherine, 1896-1963.	PR6003.U45
Burdick, Eugene.	none
Burford, Lolah.	PS3552.U714
Burger, Dionys.	none
Burger, Neal R.	none
Burgess, Anthony, 1917-	PR6052.U638 [Z8132.2]
Burgess, Eric, 1912-	PR6052.U639
Burgess, Gelett, 1866-1951.	PS3503.U6
Burgess, Mason.	none
Burgess, Michael, 1948-	PS3568.E4754 [Z8736.47]
Burgess, Scott Alan, 1964-	none
Burgo, Joseph.	none
Burke, Jonathan—see: Burke, John Frederick, 1922-	
Burke, John Frederick, 1922-	PR6003.U54
Burkett, William R.	none
Burks, Arthur J., 1898-	none
Burley, W. J. (William John)	PR6052.U647
Burman, Ben Lucien, 1895-	PS3503.U6245
Burnett, Virgil.	PR9199.3.B7917
Burnford, Sheila Every.	PR9199.3.B792
Burnham, Jeremy.	none

Burns, Jim.	PR6052.U66
Burns, Richard, 1958-	none
Burrage, A. Harcourt.	none
Burrage, Alfred McLelland.	PR6003.U566
Burroughs, Edgar Rice, 1875-1950.	PS3503.U687 [Z8136.15]
Burroughs, John Coleman.	none
Burroughs, William S., 1914-	PS3552.U75 [Z8136.17]
Burton, Elizabeth, 1907-	PR9199.3.B796
Busby, F. M.	PS3552.U79
Bushyager, Linda E.	none
Butler, David.	none
Butler, Joan, 1905-	none
Butler, Octavia E.	PS3552.U827
Butler, Samuel, 1835-1902.	PR4349.B7
Butterworth, Michael, 1924-	PR6052.U9
Butterworth, W. E. (William Edmund), 1929-	none
Buxton, Meg.	PR6052.U93
Buzzati, Dino, 1906-1972.	PQ4807.U83
Byers, Edward A.	none
Byrne, Stuart J.	none
Cabell, James Branch, 1879-1958.	PS3505.A153 [Z8139.7]
Cadigan, Pat.	none
Cady, Jack, 1932-	PS3553.A315
Caidin, Martin, 1927-	PS3553.A38
Caine, Jeffrey, 1944-	PR6053.A35
Caird, Janet.	PR6053.A36
Caldecott, Moyra.	PR6053.A3765
Calder, Nigel.	none
Caldwell, Steven, 1947-	PR6053.A378
Caldwell, Taylor, 1900-	PS3505.A364
Calif, R. C.	none
Calisher, Hortense.	PS3553.A4
Callahan, Jay.	none
Callahan, William—see: Gallun, Raymond Z., 1910-	
Callenbach, Ernest.	PS3553.A424
Callin, Grant.	none
Calvino, Italo.	PQ4809.A45
Cameron, Eleanor, 1912-	none
Cameron, Ian, 1924-	PR9619.3.P3
Cameron, Kenneth M., 1931-	PS3553.A4335
Cameron, Lou, 1924-	PS3553.A434
Campbell, Herbert James.	none
Campbell, John Wood, 1910-1971.	PS3553.A47

Campbell, Marion, 1919-	PR6053.A488
Campbell, Ramsey, 1946-	PR6053.A4855
Campton, David.	PR6053.A49
Cannon, P. H. (Peter H.)	PS3553.A529
Canty, Thomas.	none
Capek, Josef, 1887-1945.	PG5038.C27
Capek, Karel, 1890-1938.	PG5038.C3 [Z8145.13]
Capon, Paul, 1912-	PR6005.A4868
Caraker, Mary.	none
Caras, Roger A.	PS3553.A64
Card, Orson Scott.	PS3553.A655
Carew, Henry.	PR6005.A4896
Carew, Jan R.	PR9320.9.C29
Carey, Diane.	none
Carey, Peter.	PR9619.3.C36
Carl, Lillian Stewart.	none
Carlile, Clancy, 1930-	PS3553.A689
Carlock, Lynn.	none
Carlsen, Chris.	none
Carlsen, Ruth Christoffer.	none
Carlson, Dale Bick.	none
Carlson, Danny.	none
Carlson, William K.	PS3553.A735
Carlton, Roger.	none
Carlyon, Richard.	none
Carmer, Carl Lamson, 1893-	PS3505.A7265
Caro, Dennis R.	PS3553.A7585
Carpenter, Christopher.	none
Carpenter, Elmer J.	none
Carpenter, Leonard.	none
Carpentier, Alejo, 1904-	PQ7389.C26
Carpozi, George.	none
Carr, Jayge.	PS3553.A7629
Carr, John Dickson, 1906-1977.	PS3505.A763
Carr, John F.	none
Carr, Robert Spencer, 1909-	none
Carr, Terry.	PS3553.A7634
Carrel, Mark—see: Paine, Lauran.	
Carrigan, Nancy.	none
Carrigan, Richard.	none
Carrington, Grant.	PS3505.A77524
Carris, Joan Davenport.	none
Carroll, Gladys Hasty, 1904-	PS3505.A77533
Carroll, Jonathan, 1949-	PS3553.A7646
Carroll, Lewis, 1832-1898.	PR4611-4612

	[Z8234.8]
Carter, Angela, 1940-	PR6053.A73
Carter, Brian, 1937-	PR6053.A733
Carter, Bruce—see: Hough, Richard Alexander, 1922-	
Carter, Carmen.	none
Carter, Diana.	PR6053.A735
Carter, John Franklin, 1897-1967.	PS3505.A7922
Carter, Lin.	PS3553.A7823
Carter, Noel Vreeland.	none
Carter, R. M. H.	none
Cartmill, Cleve.	none
Carver, Jeffrey A.	PS3553.A7892
Case, David, 1937-	PS3553.A79
Casewit, Curtis W.	none
Cassiday, Bruce.	none
Cassidy, Sylvia.	PS3553.A7953
Cassutt, Michael.	PS3553.A812
Castle, Damon.	none
Castle, Jeffery Lloyd.	none
Castle, Mort.	none
Catley, Melanie.	none
Cavanaugh, Sara.	none
Cave, Hugh B. (Hugh Barnett), 1910-	PS3505.A912
Cebulash, Mel.	none
Chalk, Gary.	none
Chalker, Jack L.	PS3553.H247
Chalmers, Garet.	none
Chambers, Aidan.	PR6053.H285
Chambers, Jane, 1937-	PS3553.H258
Chambers, Robert W. (Robert William), 1865-1933.	PS1280-1288
Chamisso, Adelbert von, 1781-1838.	PT1834
	[Z8159]
Chance, John Newton.	PR6005.H28
Chance, Jonathan—see: Chance, John Newton.	
Chandler, A. Bertram, 1912-	PR6053.H325
Chandler, Evan.	none
Channing, Mark.	PR6005.H3118
Chant, Joy.	PR6053.H3465
Chapdelaine, Perry A. (Perry Anthony)	none
Chapman, Andrew.	none
Chapman, D. D.	none
Chapman, Vera, 1898-	PR6053.H3645
Chappell, Fred, 1936-	PS3553.H298
Chappell, George Shepard, 1877-1946.	PS3505.H44
Charbonneau, Louis, 1924-	PS3575.O7
Charkin, Paul.	none

Charles, Robert—see: Smith, Robert Charles.	
Charles, Steven.	none
Charnas, Suzy McKee.	PS3553.H325
Charteris, Leslie, 1907-	PR6005.H348
	[Z8161.8]
Chase, Adam.	none
Chase, James Hadley, 1906-	PR6035.A92
Chase, Robert R.	none
Chatrian, Alexandre, 1826-1890.	none
Chayefsky, Paddy, 1923-	PS3505.H632
Cherryh, C. J.	PS3553.H358
Chesbro, George C.	PS3553.H359
Chesney, George, Sir, 1830-1895.	none
Chesnoff, Richard Z., 1937-	PS3553.H4
Chester, Deborah.	PS3553.H425
Chester, George Randolph, 1869-1924.	PS3505.H684
Chester, Michael.	none
Chester, William L., 1907-	PS3505.H713
Chesterton, G. K. (Gilbert Keith), 1874-1936.	PR4453.C4
	[Z8166.5]
Chetwin, Grace.	none
Chetwynd-Hayes, Ronald.	PR6053.H47
Chiba, Milan.	none
Childer, Simon Ian.	none
Chilson, Robert.	none
Chilton, Charles.	none
Chilton, Irma.	none
Chiu, Tony.	PS3553.H54
Choice, Leslie.	none
Christian, Catherine, 1901-	PR6005.H65
Christie, Agatha, 1891-1976.	PR6005.H66
Christopher, John.	PR6053.H75
Chronister, Alan B.	none
Church, Ralph.	none
Church, Richard, 1893-	PR6005.H8
Churchill, Reginald Charles.	none
Clagett, John.	PS3553.L217
Clark, Curt—see: Westlake, Donald E.	
Clark, Joan, 1934-	none
Clark, Ronald.	PR6053.L318
Clark, Sheila.	none
Clark, William, 1916-	PR6053.L324
Clarke, A. C. G.	none
Clarke, A. V.	none
Clarke, Arthur Charles, 1917-	PR6005.L36
	[Z8174.6]

Clarke, Boden, 1948-	PS3568.E4754
Clarke, Robert.	none
Claro, Joe.	none
Clason, Clyde B.	none
Claudy, Carl Harry, 1879-1957.	PS3505.L475
Clay, Leon.	PS3553.L34
Clayton, Donald D.	PS3553.L3874
Clayton, Jo.	none
Clemens, Rodgers.	none
Clement, Hal, 1922-	PS3505.L646 [Z8176.2]
Clement, Henry.	none
Clements, David.	none
Cleve, John—see: Offutt, Andrew J.	
Clewett, G. C.	none
Clifford, Sarah.	none
Clifton, Mark.	PS3553.L46
Cline, C. Terry.	PS3553.L53
Clingerman, Mildred.	none
Clinton, Jeff—see: Bickham, Jack M.	
Clive, Dennis—see: Fearn, John Russell, 1908-1960.	
Clough, B. W.	none
Clouston, J. Storer (Joseph Storer), 1870-	PR6005.L845
Clow, Martha deMey.	none
Clute, John, 1940-	PR9199.3.C544
Coates, Joseph K.	none
Coates, Robert M. (Robert Myron), 1897-1973.	PS3505.O1336
Coatsworth, Elizabeth Jane, 1893-	PS3505.O136
Cobban, James MacLaren, 1849-1903.	none
Coblentz, Stanton Arthur, 1896-	PS3505.O144
Cochrane, William E.	none
Cody, C. S.—see: Waller, Leslie, 1923-	
Coe, Ross Anton.	none
Coen, Franklin.	PS3505.O236
Coffey, Frank.	PS3553.O35
Coffman, Virginia.	PS3553.O415
Cogswell, Theodore R.	none
Cohen, Barbara.	none
Cohen, Barney.	PS3553.O4183
Cohen, Matt, 1942-	PR9199.3.C58
Cole, Adrian.	PS3553.O448
Cole, Allan.	none
Cole, Burt, 1930-	PS3553.O45
Cole, Everett B., 1918-	none
Coleman, James Nelson.	none
Coles, Manning, pseud.	PS3505.O285

Collier, James Lincoln, 1928-	none
Collier, John, 1901-	PR6005.O36
Collings, Michael R.	PS3553.O474696
Collins, Hunt—see: Hunter, Evan, 1926-	
Collins, Michael—see: Arden, William, 1924-	
Collins, Wilkie, 1824-1889.	PR4490-4498 [Z8184.6]
Colomb, Philip Howard, 1831-1899.	none
Colvin, James—see: Moorcock, Michael, 1939-	
Combes, Sharon.	none
Comeau, Alexander de.	PR6005.O3876
Comer, Ralph.	none
Comfort, Alex, 1920-	PR6005.O388
Comfort, Daniel, 1950-	PS3553.O4833
Compton, D. G. (David Guy), 1930-	PR6053.O45
Comstock, Jarrod.	none
Condit, Tom.	none
Condon, Richard.	PS3553.O487
Coney, Michael.	PR6053.O453
Conly, Jane Leslie.	none
Conner, Michael.	PS3553.O5118
Conner, Mike—see: Conner, Michael.	
Connolly, Eileen.	PS3553.O5134
Conquest, Robert.	PR6005.O396
Conrad, Allan.	none
Conrad, Earl.	PS3553.O518
Conrad, Paul.	PR6063.U39
Constantine, Murray, 1896-1963.	PR6005.O44
Conte, Sal.	none
Convertito, Bill.	none
Conway, Gerard F.	none
Cook, Glen.	none
Cook, Hugh, 1956-	PR9639.3.C635
Cook, Paul H.	none
Cook, Robin, 1940-	PS3553.O5545
Cook, William Wallace, 1867-1933.	PS3505.O5593
Cooke, Catherine.	none
Coon, Horace, 1897-	none
Coon, Susan.	none
Cooney, Michael, 1921-	PR6053.O53
Coontz, Otto.	none
Cooper, Bryan.	PR6053.O543
Cooper, C. Everett.	PS3568.E4754
Cooper, Clare.	none
Cooper, Colin.	PR6053.O5464
Cooper, Edmund, 1926-	PR6053.O5469

Cooper, Giles.	PR6053.O55
Cooper, Hughes.	none
Cooper, Jeffrey, 1950-	none
Cooper, Louise, 1952-	PS3553.O595
Cooper, Parley J.	PS3553.O622
Cooper, Sonni.	none
Cooper, Susan.	none
Cooper, Tom.	none
Coover, Robert.	PS3553.O633
Copeland, Lori.	none
Coppard, A. E. (Alfred Edgar), 1878-1957.	PR6005.O55 [Z8192.8]
Coppard, Audrey.	none
Coppel, Alfred.	PS3553.O64
Copper, Basil.	PR6053.O658
Corby, Adam.	none
Corby, Michael.	none
Cordell, Alexander.	PR6053.O67
Corelli, Marie, 1855-1924.	PR4504-4505
Corey, Paul, 1903-	PS3553.O646
Corlett, William.	PR6053.O7
Corley, Edwin.	PS3553.O648
Corley, James.	none
Corman, Avery.	PS3553.O649
Cornett, Robert.	none
Corren, Grace—see: Hoskins, Robert, 1933-	
Correy, Lee—see: Stine, G. Harry (George Harry), 1928-	
Corston, George.	none
Cortázar, Julio.	PQ7797.C7145
Cory, Howard L.	none
Cost, March, d. 1973.	PR6025.O7546
Costello, Matt.	none
Cotton, Donald.	none
Coulson, Juanita.	PS3553.O83
Coulson, Robert.	PS3553.O84
Couper, Stephen.	none
Courtier, Sidney Hobson.	PR6005.O817
Cover, Arthur Byron.	none
Coville, Bruce.	none
Cowley, Stewart.	PS3553.O9135
Cowper, Richard, 1926-	PR6053.O965
Cox, Erle.	PR9619.3.C644
Cox, Joan.	none
Coyne, John.	PS3553.O96
Cozzens, James Gould, 1903-	PS3505.O99 [Z8196.9]

Cradock, Fanny, 1910-	PR6053.R23
Cradock, Phyllis—see: Cradock, Fanny, 1910-	
Craigie, David—see: Craigie, Phyllis.	
Craigie, Phyllis.	none
Craine, E. J. (Edith Janice), 1881-	none
Cram, Mildred, 1889-	PS3505.R2184
Crane, Robert.	PS3513.L646
Crawford, F. Marion (Francis Marion), 1854-1909.	PS1450-1468
Craze, Anthony.	none
Creasey, John.	PR6005.R517
Crébillon, Monsieur de (Claude-Prosper Jolyot), 1707-1777.	PQ1971.C6
Crichton, Michael, 1942-	PS3553.R48
Crichton, Neil.	PR9199.3.C686
Crisp, Quentin, 1908-	PR6005.R65
Crispin, A. C.	PS3553.R519
Crispin, Edmund, 1921-1978.	PR6025.O46
Cristabel.	PS3553.R53
Crockett, S. R. (Samuel Rutherford), 1860-1914.	PR4518.C3
Croly, George, 1780-1860.	PR4518.C55
Cromie, Robert, 1856-1907.	PR4518.C554
Cross, John Keir, 1914-	none
Cross, Polton—see: Fearn, John Russell, 1908-1960.	
Crossen, Kendell Foster, 1910-	PS3505.R89224
Crowley, Aleister, 1875-1947.	PR6005.R7 [Z8201.8]
Crowley, John.	PS3553.R597
Crump, Irving, 1887-	none
Culbreath, Myrna.	none
Cullen, Brian.	PR6053.U372
Cullen, Seamus.	PS3553.U3
Cullingworth, N. J.	none
Culp, William Maurice.	none
Culver, Timothy J.—see: Westlake, Donald E.	
Cummings, M. A.	none
Cummings, Ray.	PS3505.U339
Cunningham, E. V.—see: Fast, Howard, 1914-	
Cunningham, Jere.	PS3553.U475
Curry, Jane Louise.	none
Curtis, Jack.	PR6053.U775
Curtis, Jean Louis, 1917-	PQ2605.U55
Curtis, Philip.	none
Curval, Philippe, 1929-	PQ2663.U69
Cussler, Clive.	PS3553.U75
Da Cruz, Daniel, 1921-	PS3554.A24
Dagmar, Peter.	none

Dahl, Roald.	PR6054.A35
Dain, Alex.	none
Daley, Brian.	PS3554.A417
Dalkey, Kara.	none
Dallas, Ian.	PR6054.A43
Dalmas, John.	none
Dalos, György.	PH3213.D256
Dalton.	PR4525.D1247
Dalton, John J.	PS3554.A443
Danby, Mary.	PR6054.A463
Dane, Christopher.	none
Dane, Clemence.	PR6001.S5
Daniel, Jerry C., 1937-	none
Daniel, Mark.	none
Daniels, Dorothy, 1915-	PS3554.A563
Daniels, Les, 1943-	PS3554.A5637
Daniels, Max—see: Gellis, Roberta.	
Daniels, Norman A.	none
Daniels, Philip.	PR6054.A522
Dank, Gloria Rand.	none
Dann, Jack.	PS3554.A574
Dann, Sam, 1918-	PS3554.A577
Darby, Catherine.	none
Darke, James.	none
Darlton, Clark, 1920-	PT2664.A7
Darnay, Arsen.	PS3554.A725
Daventry, Leonard.	PS3554.A913
David, Peter.	none
Davids, Hollace.	none
Davids, Paul.	none
Davidson, Avram.	PS3554.A924
Davidson, Lionel.	PR6054.A87
Davidson, Michael, 1944-	PS3554.A9257
Davies, Andrew.	PR6054.A8755
Davies, L. P. (Leslie Purnell)	PR6054.A886
Davies, Pete, 1959-	PR6054.A89144
Davies, Robertson, 1913-	PR9199.3.D3
Davies, Valentine, 1905-1961.	PS3507.A7116
Davies, W. X.	none
Davis, Elizabeth—see: Davis, Lou Ellen, 1936-	
Davis, Frederick C. (Frederick Clyde), 1902-	PS3507.A728
Davis, Gerry.	none
Davis, Grania.	PS3554.A93456
Davis, Gwen.	PS3554.A9346
Davis, Lou Ellen, 1936-	PS3554.A9355
Davis, Maggie.	none

Dawson, Les.	none
De Camp, Catherine Crook.	none
De Camp, L. Sprague (Lyon Sprague), 1907-	PS3507.E2344
De Felitta, Frank.	PS3554.E35
De Ford, Miriam Allen, 1888-1975.	PS3507.E338
De Haven, Tom.	PS3554.E1116
De la Mare, Walter, 1873-1956.	PR6007.E3 [Z8223.1]
De Larrabeiti, Michael.	PR6054.E134
De Lint, Charles, 1951-	PS3554.E11415
De Mille, James, 1837-1880.	PS1534.D3
De Paul, Don.	PS3554.E595
De Rico, Ul, 1944-	none
De Rouen, Reed.	none
De Sena, Jorge.	none
De Timms, Graeme.	none
De Vet, Charles V.	none
Dean, Pamela C.	none
Dearen, Patrick.	none
DeBolt, Adriana.	none
DeChancie, John.	none
Decker, Jake.	none
Dee, Roger, 1932-	none
Deeping, Warwick, 1877-1950.	PR6007.E25
Defoe, Daniel, 1661?-1731.	PR3400-3408 [Z8221]
Defontenay, Charlemagne Ischir, 1888-1975.	PQ2217.D617
Deighton, Len,. 1929-	PR6054.E37
Deitz, Tom.	none
Del Martia, Astron.	none
Del Rey, Lester, 1915-	PS3554.E445
Delahaye, Michael.	PR6054.E395
Delaney, Joseph H.	none
Delany, Samuel R.	PS3554.E437 [Z8223.2]
Delap, Richard.	none
Delblanc, Sven.	PT9876.14.E55
DeLillo, Don.	PS3554.E4425
Deltz, Tom.	none
DeMarinis, Rick, 1934-	PS3554.E4554
Denham, Alice.	PS3554.E53
Denis, John.	none
Dennis, Carol L.	none
Dennis, Ian, 1952-	PR9199.3.D445
Dennis, Robert C.	PS3554.E54
Dent, Lester, 1904-1959.	PS3507.E5777

Dent, Roxanne.	none
Denton, Bradley.	none
Derleth, August William, 1909-1971.	PS3507.E69 [Z8226.7]
Dermott, Vern.	none
Detzer, Diane.	none
Deutschman, Deborah.	PS3554.E913
Dever, Joe.	none
Devin, Flanna.	none
Dewdney, A. K.	none
DeWeese, Gene.	PS3554.E929
Dexter, Carmen.	none
Dexter, J. B.—see: Glasby, John.	
Dexter, Susan.	none
Dexter, William, 1909-	none
Diaman, N. A.	PS3554.I225
Diamond, Graham.	none
Dibell, Ansen.	none
DiCarlantonio, Martin.	none
Dick, Philip K.	PS3554.I3
Dick, R. A.—see: Leslie, Josephine Aimee Campbell, 1898-	
Dick-Lauder, George.	none
Dickens, Charles, 1812-1870.	PR4550-4598 [Z8230]
Dickerson, Marilyn K.	none
Dickinson, Peter, 1927-	PR6054.I35
Dicks, Terrance.	none
Dickson, Gordon R.	PS3554.I328 [Z8230.8]
Dietz, William C.	none
Dikty, T. E. (Thaddeus Eugene), 1920-	none
Dillard, J. M.	none
Dille, Flint.	none
Dinesen, Isak, 1885-1962.	PT8175.B545 [Z8105.4]
DiPego, Gerald.	PS3554.I63
Dirac, Hugh.	none
Disch, Thomas M.	PS3554.I8
Disraeli, Benjamin, Earl of Beaconsfield, 1804-1881.	PR4080-4088 [Z8232.5]
Dixon, Dougal.	none
Dixon, Roger.	PR6054.I95
Dixon, Thomas, 1864-1946.	PS3507.I93
Dobbin, Muriel.	PS3554.O145
Doctorow, E. L., 1931-	PS3554.O3
Dodderidge, Esmé.	PR6054.O34

Dodge, Michael J.	none
Doerr, Edd.	PS3554.O35
Dolan, Mike.	none
Dolinsky, Mike.	none
Domatilla, John.	PR6054.O427
Don, Ian.	none
Donaldson, Stephen R.	PS3554.O469
Donis, Miles.	PS3554.O47
Donne, Maxim—see: Duke, Madelaine.	
Donnelly, Ignatius, 1831-1901.	PS1535.D55
Donohue, Trevor.	none
Donson, Cyril, 1919-	none
Dorer, Frances.	none
Dorer, Nancy.	none
Dorman, Sonya.	PS3554.O675
Dorn, Frank.	none
Doty, Jean Slaughter, 1924-	none
Doughty, Francis Worcester, d. 1917.	PS3507.O7528
Douglas, Carole Nelson.	PS3554.O8237
Douglas, Drake.	none
Douglas, Iain.	none
DowDell, Del.	none
Downer, Ann, 1960-	none
Doxey, William.	PS3554.O974
Doyle, Arthur Conan, Sir, 1859-1930.	PR4620-4624 [Z8240]
Dozois, Gardner R.	PS3554.O98
Drake, Asa—see: Andersson, C. Dean.	
Drake, David.	PS3554.R196
Dreadstone, Carl.	none
Dreifuss, Kurt.	none
Drew, Wayland, 1932-	PR9199.3.D74
Dreyfuss, Ernst.	none
Dring, Nat.	none
Drumm, D. B.	none
Drury, Allen.	PS3554.R8
Du Bois, Theodora McCormick, 1890-	none
Du Bois, William Pène, 1916-	none
Du Maurier, Daphne, Dame, 1907-	PR6007.U47
Du Maurier, George, 1834-1896.	PR4630-4638
Duane, Diane.	PS3554.U233
DuBreuil, Linda.	none
Dudintsev, Vladimir.	PG3476.D83
Dudley, Roy C.	none
Dudley, Terence.	none
Duffus, R. L. (Robert Luther), 1888-	PS3507.U3774

Duke, Madelaine.	PR6054.U45
Dumas, Alexandre, 1802-1870.	PQ2221-2230 [Z8247]
Duncan, Dave.	none
Duncan, David, 1913-	none
Duncan, Lois, 1934-	PS3554.U464
Duncan, Robert Lipscomb, 1927-	PS3507.U629
Dunlop, Eileen.	none
Dunn, Joseph Allan Elphinstone, 1872-1941.	PR6007.U5615
Dunn, Philip.	none
Dunn, Saul—see: Dunn, Philip.	
Dunne, Thomas L.	PS3554.U4936
Dunsany, Edward John Moreton Drax Plunkett, Baron, 1878-1957.	PR6007.U6
Duprey, Richard.	PS3554.U57
Durrell, Gerald Malcolm, 1925-	PR6054.U74
Durrell, Lawrence.	PR6007.U76 [Z8250.54]
Durst, Paul.	PS3554.U695
Dvorkin, David.	PS3554.V67
Dwyer, James Francis, 1874-	PR6007.W9
Dye, Charles.	none
Dyer, Alfred.	none
Dyer, Wayne W.	PS3554.Y45
Dykewoman, Elana—see: Nachman, Elana.	
Eager, Edward.	none
Earls, Bill.	none
Earnshaw, Anthony.	none
Earnshaw, Brian.	PR6055.A74
Easton, Edward.	none
Easton, M. Coleman.	none
Eckert, Allan W.	PS3555.C55
Eddings, David.	PS3555.D38
Eddison, Eric Rucker, 1882-1943.	PR6009.D3
Eddy, Clifford Martin.	PS3509.D412
Edler, Peter, 1934-	PR9199.3.E35
Edmonds, Harry.	none
Edmondson, G. C.	PS3555.D46
Edridge, Roger.	none
Edson, John Thomas.	PR6055.D8
Edwards, Claudia J.	none
Edwards, Gawain—see: Pendray, G. Edward (George Edward), 1901-	
Edwards, Malcolm.	PR6055.D89
Edwards, Peter.	PR6055.D947
Effinger, George Alec.	PS3555.F4
Efremov, Ivan Antonovich, 1907-	PG3476.E38

Egan, Greg, 1951-	PR9619.3.E35
Egbert, H. M.—see: Emanuel, Victor Rousseau, 1879-	
Egleton, Clive.	PR6055.G55
Ehrlich, Max Simon, 1909-	PS3509.H663
Eilers, Robert.	none
Einstein, Charles.	PS3555.I58
Eisenberg, Larry.	PS3555.I8
Eisenberg, Manuel.	PS3555.I84
Eisenstein, Phyllis, 1946-	none
Eisler, Steve.	PS3555.I87
Eklund, Gordon.	PS3555.K5
Elam, Richard M.	none
Elder, Michael.	none
Eldershaw, M. Barnard, pseud.	PR9619.3.E418
Eldridge, Paul, 1888-	PS3509.L4
Eldridge, Roger.	none
Elflandsson, Galad.	PS3555.L388
Elgin, Suzette Haden.	PS3555.L42
Eliade, Mircea, 1907-	PC839.E38 [Z8258.67]
Elias, Albert J.	none
Eliott, E. C.	none
Elkin, Stanley, 1930-	PS3555.L47
Ell, Richard G.	none
Ellern, William B.	none
Elliot, Jeffrey M.	none [Z8262.55]
Elliot, John, 1918-	PR6055.L484
Elliott, Bruce.	none
Elliott, Elton T.	none
Elliott, George P., 1918-	PS3555.L58
Elliott, John.	none
Elliott, Nathan.	none
Elliott, Richard.	none
Elliott, Sumner Locke.	PR9619.3.E44
Ellis, A. C. (Albert C.)	none
Ellison, Harlan.	PS3555.L62 [Z8262.7]
Elwood, Roger.	none
Ely, Scott.	PS3555.L94
Emanuel, Victor Rousseau, 1879-	PS3509.M17
Emerson, Ru.	none
Emerson, Willis George, 1856-1918.	none
Emmerton, Anton.	none
Emms, William.	none
Emtsev, Mikhail Tikhonovich, 1930-	PG3479.7.M7

Ende, Michael.	PT2665.N27
Enderle, Judith A.	none
Endore, S. Guy, 1901-1970.	PS3509.N374
Enfield, Hugh.	none
Engdahl, Sylvia Louise.	none
Engh, M. J.	PS3555.N423
England, George Allan, 1877-1936.	PS3509.N4
England, James.	none
Englehart, Stephen.	none
English, Charles—see: Nuetzel, Charles.	
Engstrom, Elizabeth.	PS3555.N48
Enstrom, Robert.	PS3555.N762
Erckmann, Émile, 1822-1899.	PQ2238
Erckmann-Chatrian.	PQ2238
Erdman, Paul Emil, 1932-	PS3555.R4
Erickson, Paul.	none
Erickson, Steve.	PS3555.R47
Ericson, Eric, 1925-	PR6055.R5
Ernst, Paul, 1886-	none
Ernsting, Walter—see: Darlton, Clark, 1920-	
Erskine, Barbara.	PR6055.R7
Erskine, John, 1879-1951.	PS3509.R5
Erwin, Alan R.	PS3555.R92
Eshbach, Lloyd Arthur.	none
Esler, Anthony.	PS3555.S52
Estes, Rose.	none
Estey, Dale.	PR9199.3.E8
Estleman, Loren D.	PS3555.S84
Etchemendy, Nancy.	none
Etchison, Dennis.	PS3555.T35
Eulo, Ken.	none
Evans, Christopher Riche.	none
Evans, Edward Everett, 1893-	none
Evans, Ian.	none
Ewers, Hanns Heinz, 1871-1943.	PT2609.W45
Eyers, John.	PR6055.Y47
Fagundes Telles, Lygia—see: Telles, Lygia Fagundes.	
Fairbairns, Zoë.	PR6056.A48
Fairman, Paul W.	none
Falconer, Lee N.—see: May, Julian.	
Fane, Bron—see: Fanthorpe, R. Lionel.	
Fanthorpe, P. A.	PR6056.A577
Fanthorpe, R. Lionel.	none
Faraday, Robert.	none
Farca, Marie C.	PS3556.A7
Farjeon, Benjamin Leopold, 1833-1903.	PR4699.F17

Farjeon, Eleanor, 1881-1965.	PR6011.A67
Farjeon, Joseph Jefferson, 1883-	PR6011.A74
Farley, Ralph Milne.	none
Farmer, Arthur—see: Maddock, Larry.	
Farmer, Derek.	none
Farmer, Penelope, 1939-	PR6056.A677
Farmer, Philip José.	PS3556.A72
Farrar, Stewart.	PR6056.A74
Farrell, Jackson T.	none
Farren, Mick.	PR6056.A753
Farrère, Claude, 1876-1957.	PQ2611.A78
Farris, John.	PS3556.A777
Fast, Howard, 1914-	PS3511.A784
Fast, Jonathan.	PS3556.A779
Fast, Julius, 1918-	PS3556.A78
Faucette, John M.	none
Faulcon, Robert.	none
Faust, Joe Clifford.	none
Fawcett, Bill.	none
Fawcett, Edward Douglas, 1866-	PR6011.A83
Fawcett, F. Dubrez (Frank Dubrez), 1893-	none
Fear, William H.	none
Fearn, John Russell, 1908-1960.	PR6011.E295
Federbush, Arnold.	PS3556.E24
Feist, Raymond E.	PS3556.E446
Felice, Cynthia.	PS3556.E466
Fenn, Lionel—see: Grant, Charles L.	
Ferenczy, Arpad, 1877-	PH3241.F4
Ferguson, Brad.	none
Ferguson, Patricia.	PR6056.E6193
Fergusson, Bruce.	PS3556.E7215
Ferm, Betty.	PS3556.E724
Ferreira, Rick.	PR6056.E69
Fessier, Michael, 1907-	none
Fezandié, Clement.	PS3511.E95
Fiedler, Leslie A.	PS3556.I34
Field, Eugene, 1850-1895.	PS1665-1668
Field, Ruth Baker.	none
Fielding, Henry, 1707-1754.	PR3450-3458 [Z8293.72]
Figgis, Darrell, 1882-1925.	PR6011.I35 [Z8294.93]
Finch, Sheila.	none
Findley, Timothy.	PR9199.3.F52
Fine, Peter Heath.	PS3558.E266
Finlay, Winifred.	none

Finn, Ralph Leslie.	PR6011.I58
Finney, Charles G. (Charles Grandison), 1905-	PS3511.I64
Finney, Jack.	PS3556.I52
Firbank, Ronald, 1886-1926.	PR6011.I7
First, Philip.	none
Fischman, Bernard.	PS3556.I765
Fisher, David.	none
Fisher, James P.	none
Fisher, Lou.	none
Fisher, Paul R., 1960-	none
Fisher, R. L. (Robert Lynn)	PS3556.I81433
Fisher, Stephen Gould, 1912-	PS3511.I7438
Fisher, Vardis, 1895-1968.	PS3511.I744
Fisk, Nicholas.	none
Fitch, Ed.	PS3556.I8148
FitzGibbon, Constantine, 1919-	PR6011.I88
Flagg, Francis, d. 1946.	none
Flammarion, Camille, 1842-1925.	PQ2244.F9
Fleckenstein, Alfred C.	PS1679.F5
Flecker, James Elroy, 1884-1915.	PR6011.L4
Fletcher, George U.—see: Pratt, Fletcher, 1897-1956.	
Fletcher, J. S. (Joseph Smith), 1863-1935.	PR6011.L5
Flint, Homer Eon.	none
Flint, Kenneth C.	none
Fodor, R. V.	none
Follett, James, 1939-	PR6056.O44
Fonstad, Karen Wynn.	PS3556.O47
Fontana, D. C.	PS3556.O48
Fontenay, Charles L., 1917-	none
Forbes, Caroline.	none
Ford, John M.	PS3556.O712
Ford, Richard.	PR6056.O6636
Ford, Robert Curry.	none
Forest, Salambo.	PS3556.O724
Forman, James D.	PS3556.O733
Forrest, David.	PR6056.O684
Forrest, Katherine V., 1939-	PS3556.O737
Forrest, Maryann.	PR6056.O685
Forrester, John, 1943-	none
Forstchen, William R.	none
Forster, E. M. (Edward Morgan), 1879-1970.	PR6011.O58 [Z8309.3]
Fortier, Ron J.	none
Fortune, Dion.	PR6011.I72
Forward, Robert L.	PS3556.O754
Fosburgh, Liza.	none

Foster, Alan Dean, 1946-   PS3556.O756
Foster, David, 1944-   PR9619.3.F6
Foster, George Cecil, 1893-   PR6011.O65
Foster, M. A.   none
Foster, Richard, 1910-   PS3505.R89224
Fowler, Karen Joy.   none
Fowler, Sydney—see: Wright, Sydney Fowler, 1874-1967.
Fowles, John, 1926-   PR6056.O85
Fox, Gardner F.   PS3511.O9645
Fox, Peter.   none
Fox, W. Randolph.   none
Frakes, John.   none
Frakes, Randall.   none
Frame, Janet.   PR9639.3.F7
France, Anatole, 1844-1924.   PQ2254
    [Z8312.5]
Francis, Richard, 1945-   PR6056.R277
Francois, Yves Regis.   PS3556.R333
Frank, Alan G.   none
Frank, Pat, 1908-   PS3511.R255
Frankau, Gilbert, 1884-1952.   PR6011.R26
Frankau, Pamela, 1908-1967.   PR6011.R28
Franke, Herbert W., 1927-   PT2666.R3
Franklin, Jay—see: Carter, John Franklin, 1897-1967.
Franklin, K. D.   none
Frankowski, Leo A.   none
Franson, Robert Wilfred.   none
Fraser, David, 1920-   PR6056.R28645
Fraser, Ronald, Sir, 1888-   PR6011.R297
Frayn, Michael.   PR6056.R3
Frazee, Steve, 1909-   PS3556.R358
Freddi, Cris.   PS3556.R367
Frede, Richard.   PS3556.R37
Free, Colin, 1925-   PR6056.R39
Freedman, Nancy Mars.   PS3511.R418
Freeman, Gail.   none
Freeman, Maggie.   none
Freeman, Mary Eleanor Wilkins, 1852-1930.   PS1710-1713
Fremlin, Celia.   PR6056.R45
French, Robert C.   PS3556.R44
French, Paul—see: Asimov, Isaac, 1920-
Frey, James N.—see: Washburn, Mark.
Friedberg, Gertrude.   none
Friedell, Egon, 1878-1938.   PT2611.R718
Friedman, C. S.   none
Friedman, Michael Jan.   none

Friel, Arthur Olney, 1885-	none
Friend, Ed—see: Wormser, Richard Edward, 1908-	
Friend, Oscar Jerome, 1897-	none
Friesner, Esther M.	none
Friggens, Arthur.	none
Fritch, Charles E.	none
Frith, Nigel.	PR6056.R58
Fritts, William E.	none
Fritzhand, James.	PS3556.R58
Frost, Gregory.	none
Frost, Jason.	none
Fuentes, Roberto.	none
Fuller, Alvarado Mortimer, 1851-	PS1724.F28
Fuller, Roger—see: Tracy, Don, 1905-	
Funaro, Sergio, 1922-	PQ4866.U55
Funnell, Augustine.	none
Furey, Michael—see: Rohmer, Sax, 1883-1959.	
Fyfe, H. B.	none
Fyne, Neal.	PR6011.Y7
Gadallah, Leslie.	none
Gaida, Davida.	PS3557.A3516
Galbraith, John Kenneth, 1908-	PS3557.A4113
Gallagher, Stephen.	PR6057.A3893
Gallery, Daniel V.	PS3557.A412
Gallico, Paul, 1897-	PS3513.A413
Gallion, Jane.	none
Gallun, Raymond Z., 1910-	PS3557.A4167
Galouye, Daniel F.	PS3557.A42
Gammell, David.	none
Gann, Ernest Kellogg, 1910-	PS3513.A56
Ganpat—see: Gompertz, Martin Louis Alan, 1886-	
Gantz, Kenneth F. (Kenneth Franklin), 1905-	none
García Márquez, Gabriel, 1928-	PQ8180.17.A73 [Z8323.63]
Garden, Donald J.	none
Garden, Nancy.	none
Gardner, Craig Shaw.	none
Gardner, Erle Stanley, 1889-1970.	PS3513.A6322
Gardner, John, 1933-	PS3557.A712
Gardner, Martin, 1914-	PS3557.A714
Garfield, Leon.	PR6057.A636
Garis, Howard Roger, 1873-1962.	PS3513.A6418
Garlick, Nicholas.	none
Garner, Alan.	PR6057.A66
Garner, Graham—see: Rowland, Donald S..	
Garner, Rolf—see: Berry, Bryan.	

Garnett, Bill.	PS3557.A7165
Garnett, David, 1892-	PR6013.A66
Garnett, David S.	PR6057.A677
Garrett, Randall.	PS3557.A7238
Garrido, Mar.	none
Garson, Paul.	PS3557.A79
Garson, Vaseleos.	PS3513.A734
Garth, Will—see: Kuttner, Henry.	
Garton, Ray.	none
Garvin, Richard M.	PS3557.A8
Gary, Romain.	PQ2613.A58
Gaskell, Jane, 1941-	PR6057.A73
Gasperini, Jim.	none
Gat, Dimitri V., 1936-	PS3557.A85
Gatford, Ellen.	none
Gauger, Rick.	none
Gautier, Théophile, 1811-1872.	PQ2258 [Z8329]
Gawron, Jean Mark.	PS3557.A96
Geare, Michael.	PR6057.E19
Gearhart, Sally Miller, 1931-	PS3557.E2
Geary, Patricia.	PS3557.E23
Geddes, Adrienne.	none
Gedge, Pauline, 1945-	PR9199.3.G415
Gee, Maurice.	PR9639.3.G4
Geis, Richard E.	none
Geller, Stephen.	PS3557.E4
Gellis, Roberta.	PS3557.E42
Gentle, Mary.	PR6057.E525
Gentry, Curt, 1931-	none
George, Edward—see: Vardeman, Robert E.	
George, Peter, 1924-1966.	PR6057.E54
Gerberg, Mort.	none
Gerhardie, William Alexander, 1895-	PR6013.E75
Gernsback, Hugo, 1884-1967.	PS3513.E8668
Gerrold, David, 1944-	PS3557.E69
Geston, Mark S.	PS3557.E83
Gholsten, Homer N.	none
Gibbard, T. S. J.	none
Gibbons, Floyd Phillips, 1887-1939.	PS3513.I189
Gibson, Floyd.	PR6063.U39
Gibson, Miles.	PR6057.I28
Gibson, Walter Brown, 1897-	PS3513.I2823
Gibson, William, 1948-	PR9199.3.G514
Gide, André, 1869-1951.	PQ2613.I2
Giesy, John Ulrich, 1877-	none

Gilbert, C. M.	none
Gilbert, John.	PS3557.I34218
Gilbert, Stephen, 1912-	PR6013.I3363
Gilchrist, John.	none
Gilchrist, Murray, 1868-1917.	PR6013.I3373
Gilden, Mel.	none
Giles, Raymond.	none
Gilford, C. B.	PS3557.I345
Gilliland, Alexis.	none
Gillon, Diana, 1915-	none
Gillon, Meir, 1907-	none
Gilman, Charlotte Perkins, 1860-1935.	PS1744.G57
Gilman, Robert Cham—see: Coppel, Alfred.	
Gilmore, Anthony—see: Bates, Harry.	
Gilmour, William.	PS3557.I463
Gipe, George.	PS3557.I6
Girard, Kenneth.	none
Giroux, Leo.	PS3557.I73
Gladney, Heather.	none
Glasby, John.	none
Glasser, Alan.	none
Glazer, Mindy.	none
Glemser, Bernard, 1908-	PS3513.L646
Glicksman, Frank.	none
Gloag, John, 1896-	PR6013.L5
Gloss, Molly.	none
Gluckman, Janet, 1939-	PS3557.L8214
Glut, Donald F.	PS3557.L87
Gluyas, Constance, 1920-	PR6057.L87
Glynn, A. A.	none
Goble, Lou.	none
Goble, Neil.	PS3557.O217
Godwin, Parke.	PS3557.O316
Godwin, Tom.	none
Goen, Franklin.	none
Gold, H. L.	none
Goldberg, Marshall.	PS3557.O358
Goldin, Stephen.	PR9199.3.G598
Golding, Louis, 1895-1958.	PR6013.O3
Golding, Morton J.	none
Golding, William, 1911-	PR6013.O35
Goldman, Lawrence.	PS3513.O338
Goldman, William, 1931-	PS3557.O384
Goldsmith, Howard.	none
Goldstein, Lisa.	PS3557.O397
Goldstein, William.	none

Goldston, Robert C.	none
Goll, Reinhold Weimar.	none
Gompertz, Martin Louis Alan, 1886-	PR6013.O455
Goodman, Julius.	none
Gordon, Jeffie Ross.	none
Gordon, John, 1925-	none
Gordon, Rex—see: Hough, S. B. (Stanley Bennett), 1917-	
Gordon, Stuart, 1947-	PR6057.O724
Gorey, Edward, 1925-	PS3513.O614
Gormley, Beatrice.	none
Gotlieb, Phyllis, 1926-	PR9199.3.G64
Gotschalk, Felix.	none
Goudge, Eileen.	none
Goudge, Elizabeth, 1900-	PR6013.O74
Goulart, Ron, 1933-	PS3557.O85
Gould, Joan, 1927-	none
Graat, Heinrich—see: Wolk, George.	
Graham, David, 1919-	PS3557.R194
Graham, J. M.	PR6057.R236
Graham, Robert—see: Haldeman, Joe W.	
Graham, Victoria.	PS3557.R224
Graham, Winifred, 1896-	PR6005.O69
Grant, Anthony.	none
Grant, Charles L.	PS3557.R265
Grant, Gwen.	none
Grant, Joan Marshall, 1907-	PR6013.R2737
Grant, Kathryn.	none
Grant, Maxwell—see: Gibson, Walter Brown, 1897-	
Grant, Richard, 1952-	PS3557.R268
Grant, Robert, 1852-1940.	PS1760-1763
Grass, Günther, 1927-	PT2613.R338
Gratacap, L. P. (Louis Pope), 1851-1917.	none
Grautoff, Ferdinand Heinrich, 1871-1935.	PT2613.R37
Gravey, Geary.	none
Graves, Charles Larcom, 1856-1944.	PR4728.G18
Graves, Robert, 1895-	PR6013.R35 [Z8367.5]
Gray, Alasdair.	PR6057.R3264
Gray, Curme.	none
Gray, Linda Crockett.	none
Gray, Nicholas Stuart.	PR6057.R327
Grazier, James, 1916-	PS3557.R35
Greeley, Andrew M., 1928-	PS3557.R358
Green, Edith Piñero.	PS3557.R367
Green, Henry, 1905-1974.	PR6013.R416
Green, Hilary.	none

Green, I. G.	none
Green, Joseph.	PS3557.R3725
Green, Julien, 1900-	PQ2613.R3
	[Z8368.98]
Green, Kate.	PS3557.R3729
Green, Martin Burgess, 1927-	PS3557.R37515
Green, Robert.	PR6057.R35
Green, Roger Lancelyn.	PR6013.R437
Green, Roland J.	PS3557.R37535
Green, Sharon.	none
Green, Terence M.	none
Greenberg, Martin Harry.	none
Greene, Joseph Ingham, 1897-	none
Greenfield, Irving A.	PS3557.R3942
Greenhough, Terry.	none
Greenland, Colin, 1954-	none
Greenleaf, William.	none
Greenlee, Sam, 1930-	PS3557.R396
Greenwald, Harry J.	none
Greer, Tom.	PR4728.G35
Greg, Percy, 1836-1889.	PR4728.G4
Gregorian, Joyce Ballou.	none
Gregory, Guy.	none
Gregory, Jackson, 1882-1943.	PS3513.R562
Gregory, John.	none
Gregory, Julian R.	none
Gregson, Maureen.	none
Gresham, Stephen.	none
Grey, Charles—see: Tubb, E. C.	
Gribbin, John R.	none
Grice, Julia.	none
Gridban, Volsted.	none
Grieg, Francis.	none
Griffin, Brian.	none
Griffin, George M.	none
Griffin, P. M.	none
Griffin, Russell M.	none
Griffith, George Chetwynd.	PR4728.G83
Griffith, Mary, d. 1877.	PS1764.G67
Griffith, William, 1921-	none
Grimwade, Peter.	none
Grimwood, Ken.	PS3557.R497
Grinnell, David—see: Wollheim, Donald A.	
Gripe, Maria, 1923-	PT9876.17.R52
Grohskopf, Bernice.	none
Grossinger, Richard, 1944-	PS3557.R66

Grossman, Arnold.	none
Grousset, Pascal, 1844-1909.	PR4729.G24
	PQ2269.G7
Grove, Peter J.	none
Groves, J. W.	none
Grubb, Davis, 1919-	PS3513.R865
Guard, David, 1934-	PS3557.U19
Guareschi, Giovanni, 1908-1968.	PQ4817.U193
Guest, Lynn, 1939-	PS3557.U346
Guha, Anton-Andreas, 1937-	none
Guigonnat, Henri.	PQ2667.U4636
Guin, Wyman.	none
Gull, Cyril Arthur Edward Ranger, 1876-1923.	PR6013.U54
Gull, Ranger—see: Gull, Cyril Arthur Edward Ranger, 1876-1923.	
Gunn, James E., 1923-	PS3513.U797
	[Z8375.55]
Gunn, Neil Miller, 1891-1973.	PR6013.U64
Gunther, Max, 1927-	PS3557.U53
Gurdjieff, Georges Ivanovitch, 1872-1949.	none
	[Z8375.57]
Gurney, David—see: Bair, Patrick.	
Gutteridge, Lindsay, 1923-	PR6057.U84
Gygax, Gary.	none
Gysin, Brion.	PS3557.Y8
Haas, Ben.	PS3558.A17
Haas, Dorothy F.	none
Hackett, John Winthrop, Sir, 1910-	none
Hadley, Arthur Twining, 1924-	PS3558.A316
Hadley, Franklin—see: Winterbotham, Russell Robert, 1904-	
Hadley, George, d. 1798.	PR3291
Hagberg, David.	none
Haggard, H. Rider (Henry Rider), 1856-1925.	PR4731-4732
	[Z8377.5]
Hahn, Steve.	none
Haiblum, Isidore.	PS3558.A324
Haigh, Richard.	none
Haile, Terence.	none
Hailey, Johanna.	none
Halacy, D. S. (Daniel Stephen), 1919-	none
Halam, Ann.	none
Halberstam, Michael.	PS3558.A345
Haldane, Charlotte Franken, 1894-1969.	PR6015.A247
Haldane, J. B. S. (John Burdon Sanderson), 1892-1964.	PR6058.A4359
Haldeman, Jack C., 1941-	PS3558.A3525
Haldeman, Joe W.	PS3558.A353
Haldeman, Linda.	PS3558.A354

Hale, Edward Everett, 1822-1909.	PS1770-1773
Hale, John.	PR6058.A438
Hale, Michael.	none
Hales, Edward Elton Young, 1908-	PR6058.A4394
Halkin, John.	PR6058.A4445
Hall, Adam—see: Trevor, Elleston.	
Hall, Angus.	PR6058.A4447
Hall, Austin.	none
Hall, Brian P.	none
Hall, John Ryder—see: Rotsler, William.	
Hall, Manly Palmer, 1901-	PR9199.3.H3175
Hall, Norman.	none
Hall, Sandi.	PR9639.3.H26
Hallahan, William H.	PS3558.A378
Halliwell, Leslie.	none
Hallums, James R.	none
Hambly, Barbara.	PS3558.A4215
Hamilton, Alex.	PR6058.A552
Hamilton, Andrew.	none
Hamilton, Edmond, 1904-	PS3515.A42516
Hamilton, Joan Lesley.	PS3558.A4433
Hamilton, Virginia.	PS3558.A444
Hammil, Joel.	PS3558.A4488
Han, Suyin, pseud.	PR6015.A4674
Hancock, Niel.	none
Handley, Max.	PS3558.A464
Hanna, W. C.	none
Hansen, Karl.	none
Harben, William Nathaniel, 1858-1919.	PS1785-1788
Harbinson, W. A. (William Allen), 1941-	none
Harbou, Thea von, 1888-1954.	PT2615.A62
Harcourt, Glenn.	none
Hard, T. W.	PS3558.A617
Harding, Lee, 1937-	PR9619.3.H317
Harding, Richard—see: Tine, Robert.	
Hardy, Lyndon.	none
Hargreaves, H. A., 1928-	PR9199.3.H34
Harker, Kenneth.	none
Harness, Charles L.	PS3558.A62476
Harper, George W., 1927-	PS3558.A624777
Harpur, Patrick.	PR6058.A6876
Harris, Alfred, 1928-	PS3558.A633
Harris, Barbara S.	PS3558.A635
Harris, Brian.	none
Harris, Clare Winger, 1891-	none
Harris, Deborah Turner.	none

Harris, Frank, 1855-1931.	PR4759.H37
Harris, Geraldine.	none
Harris, Gordon L.	PS3558.A6446
Harris, John Beynon—see: Wyndham, John, 1903-1969.	
Harris, Johnson—see: Wyndham, John, 1903-1969.	
Harris, Larry M.—see: Janifer, Laurence M.	
Harris, MacDonald, 1921-	PS3558.E458
Harris, Marilyn, 1931-	PS3558.A648
Harris, Raymond.	none
Harris, Rosemary, 1923-	PR6058.A6915
Harris-Burland, J. B. (John Burland), 1870-1926.	PR6015.A6473
Harrison, Craig.	PR9639.3.H3
Harrison, Harry.	PS3558.A667
Harrison, M. John (Michael John)	PR6058.A6942
Harrison, Michael.	PR6058.A694
Harrison, William, 1933-	PS3558.A672
Hartley, L. P. (Leslie Poles), 1895-1972.	PR6015.A6723
Hartmann, Franz, d. 1912.	PS1839.H43
Hartridge, Jon.	PR6058.A698
Harvey, Jon M.	none
Harvey, M. Elayn (Mary Elayn)	PS3558.A719
Harvey, Norman.	none
Harvey, William Fryer, 1885-1937.	PR6015.A7
Hassler, Kenneth W. (Kenneth Wayne)	PR6058.A78
Hastings, Milo, 1884-1957.	PS3515.A8296
Hatch, Gerald.	none
Hauff, Wilhelm, 1802-1827.	PT2293
Hautala, Rick.	none
Hawdon, Robin.	PS3558.A798
Hawes, Louise.	none
Hawke, Douglas D.	none
Hawke, Simon—see: Yermakov, Nicholas.	
Hawkes, Jacquetta Hopkins, 1910-	PR6015.A792
Hawkey, Raymond.	PS3558.A822
Hawkins, Jim.	none
Hawkins, Ward.	none
Hawthorne, Julian, 1846-1934.	PS1845-1848 [Z8392.9]
Hawthorne, Nathaniel, 1804-1864.	PS1850-1898. [Z8393]
Hay, George, 1922-	none
Hay, Jacob.	PS3558.A826
Hay, John Warwick.	PR6058.A97
Hayes, Ralph.	none
Hayles, Brian, 1931-	PR6058.A9853
Haynes, Mary.	none

Hazel, Paul.	PS3558.A889
Heard, Gerald, 1889-1971.	PR6015.E19
Heard, H. F.—see: Heard, Gerald, 1889-1971.	
Hearn, Lafcadio, 1850-1904.	PS1915-1918 [Z8393.7]
Hearne, Betsy Gould.	PS3558.E2554
Heath, Peter—see: Fine, Peter Heath.	
Hecht, Ben, 1893-1964.	PS3515.E18
Heim, Michael.	PT2668.E36
Heine, William C.	none
Heinlein, Robert A. (Robert Anson), 1907-	PS3515.E288
Helfer, Andrew.	none
Helprin, Mark.	PS3558.E4775
Heming, J. W.	none
Hemingway, Amanda.	PR6058.E49188
Henderson, Dan.	none
Henderson, Zenna.	PS3558.E495
Hendrich, Paula.	none
Hendrickson, Walter B. (Walter Brookfield), 1903-	none
Hendry, Frances.	none
Henneberg, Charles.	PQ2668.E475
Henneberg, Nathalie.	PQ2668.E479
Hensley, Joe L., 1926-	PS3558.E55
Henstell, Diana.	none
Herbert, Benson.	none
Herbert, Brian.	PS3558.E617
Herbert, Frank.	PS3558.E63 [Z8398.27]
Herbert, James, 1943-	PR6058.E62
Herck, Paul van.	PT5881.18.E6
Herley, Richard, 1950-	PR6058.E65
Hernaman-Johnson, Francis, 1879-1949.	PR6015.E714
Heron-Allen, Edward, 1861-1943.	PR6015.E7145
Hersey, John, 1914-	PS3515.E7715
Hershman, Morris, 1926-	PS3558.E78
Hervey, Michael.	none
Herzog, Arthur.	PS3558.E796
Hesse, Hermann, 1877-1962.	PT2617.E85 [Z8401.3]
Hext, Harrington—see: Phillpotts, Eden, 1862-1960.	
Heydron, Vicki Ann.	none
Heym, Stefan, 1913-	PT2617.E946
Hichens, Robert Smythe, 1864-1950.	PR6015.I4
Hickey, T. Earl.	none
Hickman, Tracy.	none
Hicks, Granville, 1901-	PS3515.I253

	[Z8405]
Higgins, Margaret.	none
Higgs, Eric C.	PS3558.I3623
High, Philip E.	none
Hildebrandt, Rita.	PS3558.I38435
Hill, Albert Fay.	none
Hill, Carol.	PS3558.I3845
Hill, David Campbell.	PS3558.I3855
Hill, Douglas, 1935-	none
Hill, Ernest.	none
Hill, John.	none
Hill, Reginald.	PR6058.I448
Hill, Roger.	none
Hiller, B. B.	none
Hiller, Neil W.	none
Hilton, John, 1900-1954.	PR6015.I53
Hinchcliffe, Philip.	none
Hindle, Lee J.	none
Hinkemeyer, Michael T.	PS3558.I54
Hintze, Naomi A.	PS3558.I55
Hinz, Christopher.	PS3558.I57
Hirschfeld, Burt, 1923-	PS3558.I67
Hitchcock, Raymond.	PR6058.I7
Hjort, James William.	PS3558.J58
Hjortsberg, William, 1941-	PS3558.J6
Hoban, Russell.	PS3558.O336
Hoch, Edward D., 1930-	PS3558.O337
Hodder, William Reginald.	PR6015.O145
Hodder-Williams, Christopher, 1926-	PR6058.O267
Hodgart, Matthew John Caldwell.	PR6058.O28
Hodgell, P. C. (Patricia C.)	PS3558.O3424
Hodgson, William Hope, 1875-1918.	PR6015.O253
Hoffman, Carl.	PS3558.O34477
Hoffman, Curtis H.	none
Hoffman, Lee.	PS3558.O346
Hoffmann, E. T. A. (Ernst Theodor Amadeus), 1776-1822.	
	PT2360-2361
	[Z8411]
Hogan, James P.	PR6058.O348
Hogan, Moreland.	PS3558.O34728
Hogan, Robert J.	PS3515.O2469
Hogg, James, 1770-1835.	PR4791-4792
Holberg, Ludvig, baron, 1684-1754.	PT8070-8094
	[Z8414.2]
Holdstock, Robert.	PR6058.O442
Holland, Cecelia, 1943-	PS3558.O348

Holly, Joan C.	none
Holly, Joan Hunter.	none
Holm, Sven, 1940-	PT8176.18.O44
Holmes, Bruce T.	none
Holmes, H. H.—see: Boucher, Anthony, 1911-1968.	
Holmes, John Eric.	PS3558.O3596
Holmes, Lawrance.	PS3558.O36
Holst, Spencer.	PS3558.O39
Holt, Conrad G.—see: Fearn, John Russell, 1908-1960.	
Holt-White, William Edward Bradden, 1878-	PR6015.O48
Holzer, Hans W., 1920-	none
Honeycombe, Gordon.	PR6058.O5
Hoobler, Thomas.	none
Hood, Gwenyth.	PS3558.O54
Hoover, H. M.	none
Hopf, Alice Lightner, 1904-	PS3523.I35
Hopkins, Kenneth.	PR6015.O62
Hopkins, Robert Thurston, 1884-	none
Hopley, George, 1903-1968.	PS3515.O6455
Hoppe, Stephanie T.	none
Horler, Sydney, 1888-1954.	PR6015.O66
Horowitz, Anthony, 1955-	none
Horton, Gordon T.	none
Horvat, Dilwyn.	none
Horvitz, Leslie.	none
Horwood, William.	PR6058.O719
Hoshi, Shin'ichi, 1926-	PL852.O8
Hoskins, Robert, 1933-	PS3558.O76
Houarner, Gerard Daniel.	none
Hough, Richard Alexander, 1922-	PR6058.O82
Hough, S. B. (Stanley Bennett), 1917-	PR6058.O83
Houghton, Claude, 1889-	PR6029.L4
Houghton, Eric.	none
House, Brian.	none
Household, Geoffrey, 1900-	PR6015.O7885
Housman, Clemence.	PR4809.H17
Housman, Laurence, 1865-1959.	PR4809.H18 [Z8418.66]
Houston, David, 1938-	none
Howard, Elizabeth Jane.	PR6058.O88
Howard, Hayden.	none
Howard, Robert Ervin, 1906-1936.	PS3515.O842 [Z8419.5]
Howard, Troy—see: Paine, Lauran.	
Howatch, Susan.	PS3558.O884
Howell, Scott.	PR6063.U39

Howells, William Dean, 1837-1920.	PS2020-2038 [Z8420.25]
Howlett, Winston A.	none
Hoyle, Fred, Sir.	PR6058.O98
Hoyle, Geoffrey.	none
Hoyle, Trevor.	PR6058.O99
Hoyt, Richard, 1941-	PS3558.O975
Hruska, Alan.	PS3558.R87
Hubbard, L. Ron (La Fayette Ron), 1911-	PS3558.U23
Hubschman, Thomas.	none
Huddy, Delia.	none
Hudner, H. Kennedy.	none
Hudson, Michael.	none
Hudson, W. H. (William Henry), 1841-1922.	PR6015.U23 [Z8422]
Huff, Lawrence.	none
Hughart, Barry.	PS3558.U347
Hughes, Denis Talbot.	none
Hughes, Edward P.	none
Hughes, James, 1937-	PR6058.U36
Hughes, Monica.	none
Hughes, Riley.	none
Hughes, Robert Don, 1949-	PS3558.U389
Hughes, Rodney.	none
Hughes, Zach—see: Zachary, Hugh.	
Hulke, Malcolm.	none
Hull, Edna Mayne.	none
Hume, Fergus, 1859-1932.	PR9639.2.H84
Hunt, Charlotte.	none
Hunter, Evan, 1926-	PS3515.U585
Hunter, Mollie, 1922-	none
Huntington, Charles.	none
Huntley, Noel.	none
Huntley, Tim.	none
Hurd, Douglas, 1930-	PR6058.U7
Hurley, Maxwell.	none
Hurwood, Bernhardt J.	PS3558.U73
Huston, Ned.	none
Hutchinson, David.	PR6058.U82
Hutson, Shaun.	none
Huxley, Aldous, 1894-1963.	PR6015.U9 [Z8430.2]
Huysmans, J.-K. (Joris-Karl), 1848-1907.	PQ2309.H4 [Z8430.55]
Hyde, Christopher.	PS3558.Y36
Hyde, Shelley—see: Reed, Kit.	

Hyne, Charles John Cutcliffe Wright, 1866-1944.	PR6015.Y6
Ing, Dean.	PS3559.N37
	[Z8436.6]
Ingram, Eleanor Marie, 1886-1921.	PS3517.N435
Ingram, Tom.	PR6059.N57
Ingrid, Charles.	none
Innes, Evan.	none
Ipcar, Dahlov Zorach, 1917-	PS3559.P37
Ireland, David, 1927-	PR9619.3.I674
Irish, William, 1903-1968.	PS3515.O6455
Irving, Washington, 1783-1859.	PS2050-2098
	[Z8439.7]
Irwin, Inez Haynes, 1873-1970.	PS3517.R864
Irwin, Robert.	PR6059.R96
Irwin, Sarita—see: Zacharia, Irwin.	
Iverson, Eric—see: Turtledove, Harry.	
Jaccoma, Richard.	PS3560.A12
Jackson, Peter.	none
Jackson, Shirley, 1919-1965.	PS3519.A392
Jackson, Steve.	none
Jacobi, Carl, 1908-	PS3519.A414
Jacobs, Harvey.	PS3560.A25
Jacques, Brian.	none
Jade, Symon.	none
Jahn, Mike.	PS3560.A35
Jakes, John, 1932-	PS3560.A37
Jakober, Marie.	PR9199.3.J376
Jales, Mark.	none
James, Dakota.	PS3560.A3788
James, Donald, 1931-	PR6060.A453
James, Henry, 1843-1916.	PS2110-2128
	[Z8447]
James, Laurence.	none
James, M. R. (Montague Rhodes), 1862-1936.	PR6019.A565
	[Z8447.4]
James, R. Alan.	none
Jameson, Malcolm.	none
Jane, Fred T. (Frederick Thomas), 1865-1910.	PR6019.A684
Janifer, Laurence M.	PS3560.A52
Janvier, Thomas Allibone, 1849-1913.	PS2129.J5
Jardine, Julie Ann.	none
Jarrett, David.	none
Jarvis, Edward.	PS3560.A6
Jason, Jerry—see: Smith, George Henry, 1922-	
Javor, F. A.	none
Jay, Mel—see: Fanthorpe, R. Lionel.	

Jay, Victor.	none
Jefferies, Mike.	none
Jefferies, Richard, 1848-1887.	PR4822-4823
	[Z8451.4]
Jenkins, Will, 1896-	PS3519.E648
Jenner, Janann V.	PS3560.E516
Jennings, Jan.	none
Jennison, John W.	none
Jensen, Johannes V. (Johannes Vilhelm), 1873-1950.	PT8175.J5
	[Z8453.5]
Jensen, Ruby Jean.	none
Jenson, Martin.	none
Jeppson, J. O.	PS3560.E6
Jerome, Owen Fox—see: Friend, Oscar Jerome, 1897-	
Jerslid, P. C. (Per Christian), 1935-	PT9876.2.E7
Jeschke, Wolfgang.	PT2670.E75
Jeter, K. W.	PS3560.E85
Jeury, Michel.	PQ2670.E8
Joëls, Kerry Mark, 1931-	PS3560.O245
Johansen, Iris.	none
Johannesson, Olof—see: Alfvén, Hannes, 1908-	
Johns, Marston—see: Fanthorpe, R. Lionel.	
Johns, W. E. (William Earl), 1893-1968.	PR6019.O3914
Johnson, Annabel, 1921-	none
Johnson, Denis, 1949-	PS3560.O3745
Johnson, Edgar, 1912-	none
Johnson, George Clayton.	none
Johnson, James B.	none
Johnson, Ken—see: Johnson, Kenneth Rayner.	
Johnson, Kenneth Rayner.	PR6060.O344
Johnston, J. M.	none
Johnston, Velda.	PS3560.O394
Johnston, William, 1924-	PS3560.O395
Johnstone, Charles, 1719?-1800?	PR3539.J25
Johnstone, William W.	none
Jones, Dennis Feltham.	PR6060.O496
Jones, Diana Wynne.	none
Jones, Douglas C.	PS3560.O478
Jones, Glyn, 1905-	PR6060.O516
Jones, Gwyneth.	none
Jones, J. A.	none
Jones, J. Jeff.	none
Jones, L. Q.	none
Jones, Langdon, 1942-	PR6060.O54
Jones, Neil R.	PS3560.O523
Jones, Raymond F., 1915-	PS3560.O5247

Jones, Robert F., 1934-	PS3560.O526
Jones, Tristan, 1924-	PR6060.O59
Jong, Erica.	PS3560.O56
Jordan, G. P.	none
Jordan, Robert.	PS3560.O7617
Jorgensen, Ivar—see: Fairman, Paul W.	
Jorgenson, Ivar—see: Silverberg, Robert.	
Joron, Andrew.	PS3560.O766
Joseph, Franz.	none
Joseph, M. K.	PR9639.3.J65
Judd, Cyril.	none
Juster, Norton, 1929-	PS3560.U8
Kafka, Franz, 1883-1924.	PT2621.A26 [Z8459.28]
Kagan, Janet.	PS3561.A363
Kahn, James.	PS3561.A37
Kainen, Ray.	PS3561.A414
Kalnen, Ray—see: Kainen, Ray.	
Kamin, Nick.	none
Kaminski, Raymond.	none
Kane, Gil.	none
Kane, Pablo—see: Zachary, Hugh.	
Kaner, Hyman.	none
Kangilaski, Jaan, 1936-	PS3561.A473
Kanto, Peter—see: Zachary, Hugh.	
Kantor, MacKinlay, 1904-	PS3521.A47
Kapp, Colin.	PR6061.A58
Kapralov, Yuri.	PS3561.A573
Karinthy, Frigyes, 1887-1938.	PH3281.K24
Karl, Jean.	none
Karlins, Marvin.	PS3561.A63
Karp, David, 1922-	none
Karr, Phyllis Ann.	PS3561.A693
Kastle, Herbert D.	PS3561.A7
Katz, Steve, 1935-	PS3561.A774
Kavan, Anna, 1904-1968.	PR6009.D63
Kay, Guy Gavriel.	PR9199.3.K39
Kaye, Marilyn.	none
Kaye, Marvin.	PS3561.A886
Kea, Neville.	none
Keith, William H.	none
Kelleam, Joseph E., 1913-	PS3521.E355
Kelleher, Victor, 1939-	PR9619.3.K454
Keller, David Henry, 1880-1963.	PS3521.E356
Kellerhals-Stewart, Heather.	none
Kelley, Leo P.	PS3561.E388

Kelley, Thomas P.	PR9199.3.K415
Kellogg, M. Bradley.	none
Kelly, David J.	none
Kelly, James P. (James Patrick)	PS3561.E3942
Kelly, Robert, 1935-	PS3561.E397
Kelman, Judith.	none
Kendall, Carol, 1917-	none
Kendall, Gordon.	none
Kendall, Mark.	none
Keneally, Thomas.	PR9619.3.K46
Kennealy, Patricia.	none
Kennedy, Leigh, 1951-	PS3561.E4266
Kennedy, Richard, 1932-	none
Kenney, Douglas C.	none
Kent, Philip—see: Bulmer, Kenneth, 1921-	
Kent, Saul.	none
Kenton, L. P.—see: Fanthorpe, R. Lionel.	
Kenyon, Ernest M.	none
Kerby, Susan Alice—see: Burton, Elizabeth, 1907-	
Kern, Gary.	PS3561.E573
Kern, Gregory—see: Tubb, E. C.	
Kernaghan, Eileen.	none
Kernahan, Coulson, 1858-1943.	none
Kerr, Katharine.	PS3561.E642
Kerr, Michael—see: Hoskins, Robert, 1933-	
Kerruish, Jessie Douglas.	none
Kersh, Gerald, 1911-1968.	PR6021.E743
Keshishian, John M., 1923-	none
Kessel, John.	none
Kesterton, David, 1948-	PR9199.3.K428
Kesteven, G. R.	none
Key, Alexander, 1904-	none
Key, Ted.	none
Keyes, Daniel.	PS3561.E769
Kidd, Ronald.	none
Kidd, Virginia.	none
Kidde, Janet—see: Wolk, George.	
Kilian, Crawford, 1941-	PR9199.3.K43
Killough, Lee.	none
Killus, James.	none
Kilworth, Garry.	PR6061.I39
Kimberly, Gail.	none
Kimbriel, Katharine Eliska.	none
Kimbro, John M., 1929-	PS3561.I417
King, Albert.	PR6063.U39
King, Bernard.	PR6061.I435

King, Christopher.	PR6063.U39
King, David, 1960-	none
King, Harold, 1945 Feb. 27-	PS3561.I476
King, John.	none
King, Stephen, 1947-	PS3561.I483
	[Z8464.47]
King, Tabitha.	PS3561.I4835
King, Tappan.	none
King, Vincent.	PR6061.I49
Kingsbury, Donald, 1929-	PS3561.I487
Kingsmill, Hugh, 1889-1949.	PR6023.U24
Kinross, Albert, 1870-	none
Kinsella, W. P.	PR9199.3.K443
Kipling, Rudyard, 1865-1936.	PR4850-4858
Kippax, John.	none
Kirban, Salem.	PS3561.I65
Kirk, Douglas.	none
Kirk, Hyland Clare, 1846-1917.	PS2189.K4
Kirk, Richard.	none
Kirk, Russell.	PS3521.I665
	[Z8465.37]
Kirst, Hans Helmut, 1914-	PT2621.I76
Klaper, Steven.	none
Klass, Philip, 1920-	PS3561.L25
Klein, Daniel M.	PS3561.L344
Klein, Gérard, fl. 1958-	PQ2671.L4
Klein, Robin.	none
Klein, T. E. D.	PS3561.L374
Kleinbaum, N. H.	none
Kline, Otis Adelbert.	PS3521.L624
Klise, Thomas S.	PS3561.L53
Klyne, Karl.	none
Kneale, Nigel.	PR6021.N413
Knebel, Fletcher.	PS3561.N4
Knerr, Michael.	none
Knight, Damon Francis, 1922-	PS3561.N44
Knight, Mallory T.—see: Hurwood, Bernhardt J.	
Knight, Norman L.	none
Knobel, Philip.	none
Knott, Bill, 1927-	PS3561.N645
Knowles, Vernon, 1899-	PR6021.N5
Knox, Calvin M.—see: Silverberg, Robert.	
Knox, Hugh.	PS3561.N687
Koch, Eric, 1919-	PR9199.3.K6
Koestler, Arthur, 1905-	PR6021.O4
	[Z8467.1774]

Kolupaev, Viktor Dmitrievich, 1936-	PG3482.7.L8
Koman, Victor.	PT2671.O425
Konvitz, Jeffrey.	PS3561.O53
Koontz, Dean R. (Dean Ray), 1945-	PS3561.O55
Kornbluth, C. M. (Cyril M.), 1924-1958.	PS3561.O67
Koster, R. M., 1934-	PS3561.O84
Kotani, Eric.	none
Kotlan, C. M.	none
Kotzwinkle, William.	PS3561.O85
Kraft, David Anthony.	none
Kramer, Dana.	none
Kramer, Kathryn.	PS3561.R2515
Kranz, E. Kirker.	none
Krensky, Stephen.	none
Krentz, Jayne Ann.	none
Kress, Nancy.	PS3561.R46
Kring, Michael.	none
Kropp, Lloyd.	PS3561.R6
Kruchten, Marcia.	none
Kubasch, Heike.	none
Kube-McDowell, Michael P.	none
Kubin, Alfred, 1877-1959.	PT2621.U1147
Kummer, Frederic Arnold, 1873-1943.	PS3521.U65
Kunetka, James W., 1944-	PS3561.U448
Kurland, Michael.	PS3561.U647
Kurtén, Björn.	PT9876.21.U7
Kurtz, Katherine.	PS3561.U69
	[Z8468.64]
Kushner, Ellen.	PR6061.U77
Kuttner, Henry.	PS3521.U87
	[Z8468.79]
Kyle, David A.	none
La Motte-Fouqué, Friedrich Heinrich Karl, Freiherr de, 1777-1843.	PT2389
La Salle, Victor.	none
La Spina, Greye, 1880-	none
Lackey, Mercedes.	none
Lafferty, R. A.	PS3562.A28
	[Z8470.85]
Lagerkvist, Pär, 1891-1974.	PT9875.L2
	[Z8470.96]
Laidlaw, Marc.	PS3562.A333
Laing, Alexander, 1903-	PS3523.A357
Lake, David J.	PR9619.3.L3
Lamb, Harold, 1892-1962.	PS3523.A4235
Lamb, Hugh.	none

Lambe, Dean R.	none
Lambert, William J.	none
Lamm, Richard D.	PS3562.A4643
Lamont, Gil.	none
Lampton, Christopher.	PS3562.A466
Lance, Kathryn.	none
Lancour, Gene.	PS3562.A467
Land, Jon.	none
Landis, Arthur H., 1917-	none
Landolfi, Tommaso, 1908-	PQ4827.A57
Landsman, Sandy.	none
Lane, Jeremy.	none
Lang, Allen Kim, 1928-	none
Lang, Andrew, 1844-1912.	PR4876-4877 [Z8481.7]
Lang, Simon.	none
Langart, Darrel T.—see: Garrett, Randall.	
Lange, Oliver.	PS3562.A485
Langelaan, Georges.	none
Langford, David.	none
Langguth, A. J., 1933-	PS3562.A49
Lanier, Sterling E.	PS3562.A52
Lanning, George, 1925-	none
Lantz, Fran.	none
Large, Ernest Charles.	PR6023.A655
Larson, Glen A.	none
Larson, Majliss.	none
Laski, Marghanita, 1915-	PR6023.A72
Lasswitz, Kurd, 1848-1910.	PT2390.L9
Latham, Philip—see: Richardson, Robert S. (Robert Shirley), 1902-	
Latimer, John, 1937-	PR9199.3.L327
Laubenthal, Sanders Anne.	none
Laumer, Keith, 1925-	PS3562.A84
Laumer, March.	none
Laurens, Marshall.	none
Lauria, Frank.	PS3523.A828
Laurie, André—see: Grousset, Pascal, 1844-1909.	
Lavers, Norman.	PS3562.A8484
Lawhead, Steve.	PS3562.A865
Lawrence, D. H. (David Herbert), 1885-1930.	PR6023.A93 [Z8480.5]
Lawrence, David E.	PS3562.A9118
Lawrence, J. A.	none
Lawrence, Louise, 1943-	none
Lawrence, Margery H.	PR6023.A935
Laws, Stephen.	PR6062.A933

Laymon, Richard.	none
Lazarus, Keo Felker.	none
Le Fanu, Joseph Sheridan, 1814-1873.	PR4879.L7
Le Guin, Ursula K., 1929-	PS3562.E42
	[Z8495.88]
Le Queux, William, 1864-1927.	PR6023.E75
Le Sage, Alain René, 1668-1747.	PQ1997
	[Z8503]
Leader, Mary.	PS3562.E18
Leahy, John Martin, 1886-	none
LeBaron, Anthony—see: Laumer, Keith, 1925-	
Lee, Elsie.	PS3562.E345
Lee, John, 1931-	PS3562.E3537
Lee, Tanith.	PR6062.E4163
Lee, Vernon, 1856-1935.	PR5115.P2
Lee, Walt.	none
Lee, Wayne C.	PS3523.E34457
Leiber, Fritz, 1910-	PS3523.E4583
Leiber, Justin.	none
Leichter, Larry R.	none
Leigh, Stephen.	none
Leighton, Edward.	none
Leimas, Brooke.	none
Leinster, Murray, 1896-	PS3519.E648
Lem, Stanislaw.	PG7158.L39
L'Engle, Madeleine.	PS3523.E55
Leokum, Leonard.	none
Leonard, George H.	none
Leonard, Raymond.	none
Léourier, Christian, 1948-	PQ2672.E625
Lerman, Rhoda.	PS3562.E68
Lerner, Richard A. (Richard Alan), 1938-	none
Leroe, Ellen, 1949-	PS3562.E76
Leroux, Gaston, 1868-1927.	PQ2623.E6
Leslie, Desmond, 1921-	PR6062.E78
Leslie, Josephine Aimee Campbell, 1898-	PR6023.E774
Leslie, Peter, 1922-	none
Lesser, Milton—see: Marlowe, Stephen, 1928-	
Lessing, Doris May, 1919-	PR6023.E833
Lester, Andrew.	none
Leven, Jeremy.	PS3562.E866
Levin, Betty.	none
Levin, Ira.	PS3523.E7993
Levin, Meyer, 1905-	PS3523.E7994
	[Z8504.353]
Levy, David, 1913-	PS3562.E927

Levy, Edward.	PS3562.E92715
Lewin, Leonard C.	PS3562.E928
Lewis, C. S. (Clive Staples), 1898-1963.	PR6023.E926
	[Z8504.37]
Lewis, Irwin.	none
Lewis, M. G. (Matthew Gregory), 1775-1818.	PR4887-4888
Lewis, Richard, 1935-	PS3562.E972
Lewis, Roy, 1913-	PR6062.E954
Lewis, Sinclair, 1885-1951.	PS3523.E94
	[Z8504.38]
Lewis, Wyndham, 1882-1957.	PR6023.E97
	[Z8504.39]
Lewitt, S. N.—see: Lewitt, Shariann.	
Lewitt, Shariann.	none
Leyton, E. K.	none
Lichtenberg, Jacqueline.	PS3562.I3
Lieberman, Robert.	PS3562.I44
Lief, Evelyn.	none
Lientz, Gerald.	none
Light, John.	none
Lightner, A. M.—see: Hopf, Alice Lightner, 1904-	
Lindholm, Megan.	none
Lindsay, David, 1876-1945.	PR6023.I58115
Linehan, L.	none
Ling, Peter.	none
Linklater, Eric, 1899-1974.	PR6023.I582
Linssen, John.	PS3562.I552
Linzner, Gordon, 1949-	PS3562.I565
Lionel, Robert—see: Fanthorpe, R. Lionel.	
Lippincott, David.	PS3562.I58
Liquori, Sal.	none
Little, Jane.	none
Lively, Penelope, 1933-	PR6062.I89
Livesey, John.	none
Livingston, Harold.	PS3562.I934
Livingston, Marjorie, 1893-	none
Livingstone, Ian.	none
Livoni, Cathy, 1956-	none
Ljoka, Dan.	none
Llewellyn, Edward.	none
Lloyd, Jeremy.	PR6062.L64
Lloyd, John Uri, 1849-1936.	PS3523.L64
Llywelyn, Morgan.	PS3562.L94
Lobel, Brana.	PS3562.O2
Locke, Richard Adams, 1800-1871.	PS2248.L835
Lofts, Norah, 1904-	PR6023.O35

Logan, Charles.	PR6062.O37
Logsdon, Syd.	none
London, Jack, 1876-1916.	PS3523.O46
	[Z8514.6]
Long, Charles R.	none
Long, Doug.	none
Long, Frank Belknap, 1903-	PS3523.O465
Long, John.	none
Long, Lyda Belknap—see: Long, Frank Belknap, 1903-	
Longmate, Norman, 1925-	PR6062.O5155
Longo, Chris.	none
Longyear, Barry B.	PS3562.O53
Loomis, Noel M., 1905-	none
Lopez, Enrique Hank.	none
Loraine, Philip, pseud.	PR6062.O67
Lord, Jeffrey.	none
Lornquest, Olaf.	none
Lorrah, Jean.	PS3562.O767
Lortz, Richard.	PS3562.O77
Lory, Robert.	PS3562.O78
Lottman, Eileen.	PS3562.O79
Lovecraft, H. P. (Howard Phillips), 1890-1937.	PS3523.O833
	[Z8520.9]
Lovejoy, Jack.	none
Lovell, Marc.	PR6062.O853
Lovelock, James.	none
Lovin, Roger.	PS3562.O875
Low, A. M. (Archibald Montgomery), 1888-	none
Lowenthal, Mark M.	none
Lowndes, Belloc, Mrs.—see: Lowndes, Marie Adelaide Belloc.	
Lowndes, Marie Adelaide Belloc, 1868-1947.	PR6023.O95
Lowndes, Robert W.	none
Lucarotti, John.	none
Lucas, E. V. (Edward Verrall), 1868-1938.	PR6023.U24
Lucas, George.	PS3562.U234
Lucas, John Meredyth—see: Tracy, Don, 1905-	
Ludlam, Harry.	none
Ludwig, Edward W.	none
Luenn, Nancy.	none
Luke, Thomas—see: Masterton, Graham.	
Lukeman, Tim.	PS3562.U465
Lukodianov, Isai Borisovich, 1913-	none
Lumley, Brian.	PR6062.U45
Lundwall, Sam J., 1941-	PT9876.22.U62
Lunn, Janet Louise Swoboda, 1928-	none
Lupoff, Richard A., 1935-	PS3562.U6

Lustbader, Eric Van.	PS3562.U752
Luther, Ray—see: Sellings, Arthur, 1921-	
Lyall, D. K.	none
Lydecker, John.	none
Lyle, Peter.	none
Lymington, John.	PR6005.H28
Lynch, Miriam.	PS3562.Y434
Lynds, Dennis—see: Arden, William, 1924-	
Lynn, Elizabeth A.	PS3562.Y443
Lyon, Richard K.	none
Lytle, Andrew Nelson, 1902-	PS3523.Y88 [Z8530.57]
Lytton, Edward Bulwer Lytton, Baron, 1803-1873.	PR4900-4948
MacApp, C. C.	none
Macaulay, David.	none
Macauley, Robie.	PS3563.A25315
MacAvoy, R. A.	none
Maccabee, John.	none
MacCloud, Malcolm.	none
MacConnell, Colum.	none
MacCreigh, James—see: Pohl, Frederik.	
Macdonald, Andrew.	PS3563.A2747
MacDonald, George, 1824-1905.	PR4965-4969
MacDonald, John D. (John Dann), 1916-	PS3563.A28 [Z8538.383]
MacDonald, Philip.	PR6025.A2218
Mace, David.	none
Macey, Peter.	PR6063.A214
Macgregor, James Murdoch.	PR6063.A234
MacGregor, Loren.	none
Machen, Arthur, 1863-1947.	PR6025.A245 [Z8533.75]
MacIsaac, Frederick John, 1886-	none
Mackelworth, R. W.	none
Mackenroth, Nancy.	none
Mackenzie, Compton, Sir, 1883-1972.	PR6025.A2526 [Z8535.2]
Mackey, Mary.	PS3563.A3165
Macksey, Kenneth.	none
MacLean, Katherine.	PS3563.A31799
MacLeish, Roderick, 1926-	PS3563.A3183
MacLennan, Hugh, 1907-	PR9199.3.M334
MacLennan, Phyllis.	PS3563.A3185
MacLeod, Charlotte.	PS3563.A31865
Macleod, Fiona—see: Sharp, William, 1855-1905.	
MacLeod, Sheila.	PR6063.A253

MacManus, Yvonne.	PS3563.A31885
MacMillan, Ian T.	PS3563.A318955
Macnie, John.	PS2359.M587
MacVicar, Angus, 1908-	PR6025.A34
Maddock, Larry.	none
Maddox, Carl—see: Tubb, E. C.	
Maddux, Rachel, 1913-	PS3563.A3395
Mader, Friedrich Wilhelm, 1866-	PT2625.A24
Madle, Robert.	none
Madlee, Dorothy H.	none
Madsen, Axel.	PS3563.A343
Maggin, Elliot S.	none
Mahr, Kurt.	none
Mahy, Margaret.	none
Maikowski, Michael F.	none
Mailer, Norman.	PS3525.A4152 [Z8543.65]
Maine, Charles Eric—see: McIlwain, David, 1921-	
Major, H. M.	none
Malamud, Bernard.	PS3563.A4 [Z8544.57]
Malcolm, Donald.	none
Malec, Alexander.	none
Malone, Adrian.	PS3563.A4322
Maloney, Mack.	none
Malzberg, Barry N.	PS3563.A434
Mandino, Og.	PS3563.A464
Manley, Mary de la Rivière, 1663-1724.	PR3545.M8
Mann, Jack—see: Vivian, Evelyn Charles H.	
Mann, Phillip.	PR9639.3.M256
Mann, Thomas, 1875-1955.	PT2625.A44 [Z8547.41]
Mannes, Marya.	PS3525.A542
Manning, Laurence.	none
Manning, Rosemary.	PR6063.A385
Mannon, Warwick—see: Hopkins, Kenneth.	
Mano, D. Keith.	PS3563.A56
Mantley, John.	none
Manvell, Roger, 1909-	none
Marasco, Robert.	PS3563.A63
Marcelin, Pierre, 1908-	none
March, Gene.	none
Marconi, David.	none
Marcus, Robert B.	none
Marden, William.	PS3563.A644
Margroff, Robert E.	none

Mark, Jan.	none
Marks, Alan.	none
Marl, David J.	none
Marlowe, Stephen, 1928-	PS3563.A674
Marney, Dean, 1952-	none
Marquis, Don, 1878-1937.	PS3525.A67
Marryat, Frederick, 1792-1848.	PR4975-4979
Marsh, Geoffrey, 1912-	PS3563.A7145
Marsh, Richard, d. 1915.	PR6025.A645
Marshak, Sondra.	none
Marshall, Bruce, 1899-	PR6025.A654
Marshall, Deborah A.	none
Marshall, Edison, 1894-1967.	PS3525.A7266
Marshall, Sidney John, 1866-	PS3525.A72783
Marshall, William Leonard, 1944-	PR9619.3.M275
Marsten, Richard—see: Hunter, Evan, 1926-	
Martel, Suzanne Chouinard.	PQ3919.2.M3
Marten, Jacqueline.	none
Marter, Ian.	none
Martin, Carl.	none
Martin, George R. R.	PS3563.A7239
Martin, Graham Dunstan.	none
Martin, Jack—see: Etchison, Dennis.	
Martin, Jack, 1938-	PS3563.A7242
Martin, John Joseph, 1893-	PS3563.A72437
Martin, Les, 1934-	none
Martin, Lori.	PS3563.A72493
Martin, Marcia, 1918-	none
Martin, Rodney.	none
Martin, Russ.	PS3563.A7284
Martine-Barnes, Adrienne.	none
Martini, Virgilio.	PQ4828.A782
Marvell, Andrew.	none
Masefield, John, 1878-1967.	PR6025.A77 [Z8553.6]
Masello, Robert.	none
Mason, A. E. W. (Alfred Edward Woodley), 1865-1948.	PR6025.A79
Mason, Anne (Laura Anne)	none
Mason, David.	none
Mason, Douglas R.	PR6063.A76
Massa, Jack.	none
Masson, David I.	none
Masters, Anthony, 1940-	PR6063.A83
Masters, Doug.	none
Masters, John, 1914-1983.	PS3525.A8314
Masterton, Graham.	PR6063.A834

Matheson, Richard, 1926-	PS3563.A8355
Matheson, Richard Christian.	none
Mathews, Richard, 1944-	none
Matson, Norman, 1893-	none
Matthews, Brander, 1852-1929.	PS2370-2373
	[Z8554.7]
Matthews, Rodney.	none
Maturin, Charles Robert, 1780-1824.	PR4987.M7
Matzkin, M.	none
Maugham, W. Somerset (William Somerset), 1874-1965.	PR6025.A86
	[Z8555.3]
Maurois, André, 1885-1967.	PQ2625.A95
	[Z8555.75]
Max, Nicholas.	PS3563.A894
Maxim, John R.	PS3563.A8965
Maxwell, A. E., 1944-	PS3563.A899
Maxwell, Ann.	none
Maxwell, John C.—see: Glasby, John.	
Maxxe, Robert.	PS3563.A935
May, Julian.	PS3563.A942
	[Z8557.6]
May, Karl Friedrich, 1842-1912.	PT2625.A848
May, Kenneth.	none
Mayer, Robert, 1939-	PS3563.A954
Mayhar, Ardath.	PS3563.A962
Mayhew, Vic.	PS3563.A963
Mayne, William, 1928-	none
Mazer, Norma Fox, 1931-	PS3563.A982
McAleer, Neil, 1942-	PS3563.A245
McAllister, Bruce, 1946-	PS3563.A232
	[Z8561.13]
McBain, Gordon.	PS3563.C333
McBratney, Sam.	PR6063.C3
McCaffrey, Anne.	PS3563.A255
McCammon, Robert R.	PS3563.C3345
McCarty, Dennis.	none
McCay, Claudia.	none
McClary, Thomas Calvert.	PS3525.A1514
McClintock, Michael W. (Michael William), 1942-	none
McCollum, Michael.	none
McConkey, James.	PS3563.C3435
McCoy, Glen.	none
McCrumb, Sharyn.	none
McCullough, Colleen, 1937-	PR9619.3.M32
McCutchan, Philip, 1920-	PR6063.A167
McDaniel, David.	none

McDevitt, Jack.	none
McDonald, Stephen E.	none
McDonell, Terry.	PS3563.A29143
McDowell, Michael.	none
McElroy, Joseph.	PS3563.A293
McEnroe, Richard S.	none
McEvoy, Seth.	none
McGarry, Mark J.	none
McGeary, Duncan.	none
McGhee, Edward.	none
McGill, Gordon, 1943-	PR6063.A2177
McGivern, William P.	PS3525.A236
McGowen, Tom.	none
McGregor, Don.	PS3563.C368
McGuire, John J.	none
McHargue, Georgess.	none
McHugh, Vincent, 1904-	PS3525.A2457
McIntosh, J. T.—see: Macgregor, James Murdoch.	
McIntyre, Vonda N.	PS3563.A3125
McKenna, Richard.	PS3563.A3155
McKenney, Kenneth, 1929-	PR6063.A2429
McKiernan, Dennis L., 1932-	PS3563.C376
McKillip, Patricia A.	PS3563.C38
McKinley, Robin.	none
McKinney, Jack.	none
McLaughlin, Dean.	PS3563.A31794
McLoughlin, John C.	PS3563.C385
McNab, Oliver—see: Frede, Richard.	
McNally, Clare.	none
McNeil, John.	PR6063.A2586
McQuay, Mike.	none
McQueen, Ronald A.	none
McShane, Mark, 1930-	PR6062.O853
Meacham, Beth.	none
Mead, Harold.	none
Mead, Shepherd.	PS3525.E1147
Meade, Richard—see: Haas, Ben.	
Meaney, Dee Morrison.	none
Meek, Sterner St. Paul, 1894-	none
Meier, Shirley.	none
Meldal-Johnsen, Trevor.	none
Meltzer, David.	PS3563.E45 [Z8562.57]
Meluch, R. M. (Rebecca M.)	none
Mendelsohn, Alan.	none
Mendelsohn, Felix, 1906-	PS3563.E48

Mendelson, Drew.	none
Menegas, Peter.	none
Menen, Aubrey.	PR6025.E5
Menville, Douglas Alver.	none
Merak, A. J.—see: Glasby, John.	
Mercier, Louis Sebastien, 1740-1814.	PQ2007.M6
Meredith, George, 1828-1909.	PR5000-5018 [Z8568.8]
Meredith, Richard C.	PS3563.E737
Meretzky, S. Eric.	none
Merle, Robert, 1908-	PQ2625.E5278
Merriam, Eve, 1916-	PS3525.E639
Merril, Judith, 1923-	PS3525.E643
Merritt, A.—see: Merritt, Abraham, 1882-1943.	
Merritt, Abraham, 1882-1943.	PS3525.E676
Merwin, Samuel, 1910-	none
Messmann, Jon.	none
Meyer, John Joseph, 1873-	PS2389.M5
Meyers, Richard S.	none
Meyers, Roy L.	none
Meyrick, Bette, 1931-	none
Meyrink, Gustav, 1868-1932.	PT2625.E95
Mezo, Francine.	none
Miall, Robert—see: Burke, John Frederick, 1922-	
Michaels, Barbara, 1927-	PS3563.E747
Michaels, Melisa C.	none
Michaels, Philip.	none
Miesel, Sandra, 1941-	none
Miklowitz, Gloria D.	none
Milán, Victor.	PS3563.I371568
Millard, Joseph.	none
Miller, Calvin.	PS3563.I376
Miller, George.	none
Miller, J. P. (James Pinckney), 1919-	PS3563.I397
Miller, Jimmy.	PS3563.I413
Miller, Larry.	none
Miller, P. Schuyler (Peter Schuyler), 1912-1974.	PS3525.I55727
Miller, Phyllis.	none
Miller, Richard, 1925-	PS3563.I4212
Miller, Richard DeWitt.	none
Miller, Ruth, 1921-	PR6063.I375
Miller, Walter M., 1923-	PS3563.I4215
Miller, Warren.	none
Millhauser, Steven.	PS3563.I422
Millhiser, Marlys.	PS3563.I4225
Mills, Craig.	none

Mills, Robert E.	none
Milne, Robert Duncan.	none
Minton, T. M.	none
Mirrlees, Hope.	PR6025.I79
Mitchell, Adrian, 1932-	PR6063.I77
Mitchell, Edward Page, 1852-1937.	PS3525.I9613
Mitchell, J. A.—see: Mitchell, John Ames, 1845-1918.	
Mitchell, J. Leslie—see: Mitchell, James Leslie, 1901-1935.	
Mitchell, James Leslie, 1901-1935.	PR6025.I833
Mitchell, John Ames, 1845-1918.	PS2409.M2
Mitchell, Kirk.	none
Mitchelson, Austin.	none
Mitchison, Naomi, 1897-	PR6025.I85
Modesitt, L. E.	none
Moffatt, James.	none
Moffett, Judith, 1942-	PS3563.O29
Moffitt, Donald.	PS3563.O297
Molesworth, Mrs., 1842-1921.	PR5029.M62
Molesworth, Vol.	none
Monaco, Richard.	PS3563.O515
Moncrif, Augustin Paradis de, 1687-1770.	PQ2007.M85
Monette, Paul.	PS3563.O523
Monsarrat, Nicholas, 1910-	PR6025.O36
Montana, Ron.	none
Monteleone, Thomas F.	PS3563.O542
Montgomery, R. A.	none
Moon, Sheila.	PS3563.O564
Mooney, Ted.	PS3563.O567
Moorcock, Michael, 1939-	PR6063.O59 [Z8952.53]
Moore, Arthur.	none
Moore, Brian, 1921-	PR9199.3.M617
Moore, C. L. (Catherine Lucile), 1911-	PS3563.O59
Moore, Patrick.	none
Moore, Raylyn.	PS3563.O629
Moore, Robin, 1925-	PS3563.O644
Moore, Silas.	PS3563.O66
Moore, Wallace.	none
Moore, Ward, 1903-	PS3563.O668
Mooser, Stephen.	none
Moran, Daniel—see: Vardeman, Robert E.	
Moran, Richard, 1942-	PS3563.O767
Morgan, Dan.	none
Morgan, Dave.	none
Morgenstern, S.—see: Goldman, William, 1931-	
Morhaim, Joe.	none

Morland, Dick—see: Hill, Reginald.	
Morley, Christopher, 1890-1957.	PS3525.O71
Morningstar, Ramón Sendér, 1934-	PS3563.O87196
Moroz, Anne.	none
Morrell, David.	PR9199.3.M65
Morressy, John.	PS3563.O8736
Morris, Chris, 1946-	none
Morris, Dave.	none
Morris, Janet, 1946-	PS3563.O87435
Morris, Jim, 1940-	PS3563.O87436
Morris, Kenneth, 1879-1937.	PR6025.O7527
Morris, M. E., 1926-	PS3563.O87444
Morris, Ralph, fl. 1751-	PR3605.M813
Morris, William, 1834-1896.	PR5070-5088 [Z8595]
Morris, Winifred.	none
Morrissey, Joseph Laurence, 1905-	none
Morrison, William.	none
Morrow, James, 1947-	PS3563.O876
Morse, L. A.	none
Morwood, Peter.	none
Moss, Robert, 1946-	PR6063.O83
Moss, Roger.	none
Moudy, Walter.	none
Mueller, Richard.	none
Muir, Douglas.	none
Mujica Láinez, Manuel, 1910-	PQ7797.M74
Mullally, Frederic.	PR6063.U38
Mullen, Stanley, 1911-	PS3525.U4124
Muller, John E.	none
Muller, Paul, 1924-	PR6063.U39
Munby, A. N. L. (Alan Noel Latimer), 1913-1974.	none
Mundy, Talbot, 1879-1940.	PR6025.U66
Munn, H. Warner.	PS3525.U52
Munson, Brad.	none
Murdock, M. S.	PS3563.U7253
Murnane, Gerald, 1939-	PR9619.3.M76
Murphy, Gloria.	PS3563.U7297
Murphy, Michael, 1930 Sept. 3-	PS3563.U746
Murphy, Pat.	PS3563.U748
Murphy, Robert Franklin.	none
Murphy, Shirley Rousseau.	none
Murray, Frieda A.	none
Murray, Gilbert, 1866-1957.	PR6025.U74
Musser, Joe.	PS3563.U84
Myers, Gary.	PS3563.Y37

Myers, Howard L.	none
Myers, John Myers, 1906-	PS3525.Y428
Myers, Robert John, 1924-	PS3563.Y45
Myers, Walter Dean, 1937-	none
Mylius, Ralph, 1945-	none
Myra, Harold Lawrence, 1939-	PS3563.Y7
Nabokov, Vladimir Vladimirovich, 1899-1977.	PS3527.A15 [Z8608.6]
Nachman, Elana.	PS3564.A27
Nader, George.	PS3564.A29
Naha, Ed.	none
Nahmlos, John.	none
Nathan, David, 1926-	none
Nathan, Robert, 1894-	PS3527.A74 [Z8614.8]
Nation, Terry.	PR6064.A67
Naylor, Phyllis Reynolds.	PS3564.A9
Nearing, Homer, 1915-	none
Nebrensky, Alex—see: Cooper, Parley J.	
Needleman, Jacob.	PS3564.E23
Neeper, Cary.	PS3564.E26
Neiderman, Andrew.	none
Neill, Alexander Sutherland, 1883-1973.	none
Neill, Peter, 1941-	PS3564.E3
Neill, Robert.	PR6064.E44
Nelson, John, 1947-	PS3564.E465
Nelson, Ray Faraday, 1931-	PS3564.E4745
Nesbit, E. (Edith), 1858-1924.	PR4149.B4
Nesvadba, Josef.	PG5038.N453
Neufeld, John.	PS3564.E84
Neville, Kris, 1925-	PS3564.E852
Newbolt, Henry John, Sir, 1862-1938.	PR5103.N4
Newby, P. H. (Percy Howard), 1918-	PR6064.E87
Newcomb, Simon, 1839-1909.	PS2459.N3485 [Z8621.7]
Newell, Neil K.	none
Newman, Bernard, 1897-1968.	PR6027.E914
Newman, Richard Louis.	none
Newman, Sharan.	PS3564.E926
Nichols, Leigh, 1945-	PS3561.O55
Nichols, Ruth, 1948-	PR6064.I22
Nicholson, Sam.	none
Niebelschütz, Wolf von, 1913-1960.	PT2627.I45
Niles, Douglas.	none
Nim, P. S.	none
Nimmo, Jenny.	none

Nimoy, Leonard.	PS3564.I5
Niven, Larry.	PS3564.I9
	[Z8629.3]
Noble, Mark.	none
Noël, Atanielle Annyn.	PS3564.O29
Noel, Sterling.	none
Noir, Stephard.	none
Nolan, Madeena Spray.	none
Nolan, William F., 1928-	PS3564.O39
	[Z8630.84]
Noone, Edwina—see: Avallone, Michael.	
Norden, Eric.	none
Norman, Diana.	PR6064.O73
Norman, Elizabeth, 1924-	PS3564.O564
Norman, John, 1931-	PS3564.O6
North, Andrew—see: Norton, Andre.	
North, Edmund H.	none
North, Eric.	none
North, Joan.	none
Northrup, Edwin Fitch, 1866-	PS3527.O596
Norton, Andre.	PS3527.O632
	[Z8633.2]
Norton, Mary.	none
Norvil, Manning—see: Bulmer, Kenneth, 1921-	
Norwood, Victor George Charles.	PR6064.O79
Norwood, Warren.	none
Nourse, Alan Edward.	PS3564.O8
Nowlan, Phil.	none
Noyes, Alfred, 1880-1958.	PR6027.O8
Noyes, Ralph.	none
Nuetzel, Charles.	none
Nunes, Claude.	none
Nunes, Rhoda.	none
Nyberg, Bjorn.	none
Nye, Jody Lynn.	none
Nye, Robert.	PR6064.Y4
Oakes, Philip, 1928-	PR6065.A38
Oboler, Arch, 1907-1987.	PS3529.B45
O'Brien, David.	none
O'Brien, Fitz James, 1828-1862.	PS2485
O'Brien, Flann, 1911-1966.	PR6029.N56
O'Brien, Robert C.	PS3565.B74
O'Brien, Tim.	PS3565.B75
Obruchev, V. A. (Vladimir Afanas'evich), 1863-1956.	PG3476.O17
	[Z8639.2]
Obukhova, Lydiia.	PG3484.2.B8

O'Callaghan, Maxine.	none
O'Day-Flannery, Constance.	none
Odle, E. V.	none
O'Donnell, Elliott, 1872-1965.	PR6029.D52
O'Donnell, K. M.—see: Malzberg, Barry N.	
O'Donnell, Kevin.	none
O'Donnell, Lawrence—see: Kuttner, Henry.	
Offutt, Andrew J.	PS3565.F4
O'Grady, Rohan, 1922-	PR9199.3.O343
Ohle, David.	PS3565.H6
Okun, Lawrence E., 1929-	PS3565.K8
Olden, Marc.	PS3565.L29
O'Leary, Brian, 1940-	none
Oleck, Jack.	PS3565.L4
Olemy, P. T.	none
Olesker, J. Bradford, 1949-	PS3565.L44
Oliphant, Mrs. (Margaret), 1828-1897.	PR5113-5114
Oliver, Chad, 1928-	PS3565.L458 [Z8642.76]
Oltion, Jerry B.	none
O'Neil, Dennis, 1939-	none
O'Neill, Joseph.	PR6029.N38
Onions, Oliver, 1873-1961.	PR6029.N54
Onopa, Robert.	none
Oppenheim, E. Phillips (Edward Phillips), 1866-1946.	PR6029.P5
Oppenheim, Shulamith.	none
Oram, John.	none
Orgill, Douglas, 1922-	PR6065.R68
O'Riordan, Robert.	none
Orkow, Ben.	PS3565.R57
Ormesson, Jean d', 1925-	PQ2629.R58
Ormondroyd, Edward.	none
Orr, A. (Alice)	PS3565.R68
Orr, Paul.	none
Orr, Violet.	none
Orwell, George, 1903-1950.	PR6029.R8 [Z8647]
Osborne, David—see: Silverberg, Robert.	
Osburn, Joseph.	none
O'Shea, Pat.	none
Osier, John, 1938-	PS3565.S55
Osmond, Andrew.	PR6065.S6
Ottum, Bob.	PS3565.T8
Owen, Dean.	PS3565.W53
Owen, Frank, 1893-	PS3529.W265
Owen, Richard, 1942-	PS3565.W56

Owen, Thomas, 1910-	PQ2675.W44
Owston, C. E.	none
Ozick, Cynthia.	PS3565.Z5
Packard, Edward, 1931-	none
Padgett, Lewis.	PS3521.U87
Page, Ian.	none
Page, Norvell W.	none
Page, Thomas, 1942-	PS3566.A335
Paige, Richard.	none
Pain, Barry, 1864-1928.	PR6031.A25
Paine, Albert Bigelow, 1861-1937.	PS3531.A27
Paine, Lauran.	PS3566.A34
Pal, George.	none
Palin, Michael.	PR6066.A42
Palmer, David R.	none
Palmer, Jane.	none
Paltock, Robert, 1697-1767.	PR3615.P5
Palumbo, Dennis.	none
Panati, Charles, 1943-	PS3566.A558
Pangborn, Edgar.	PS3566.A56
Panshin, Alexei, 1940-	PS3566.A58
Panshin, Cory.	none
Parenteau, Shirley.	PS3566.A646
Paris, Matthew, 1938-	PS3566.A66
Park, Paul, 1954-	PS3566.A6745
Park, Ruth.	PR9639.3.P37
Parker, Chris.	none
Parker, Richard, 1915-	PR6066.A67
Parkes, Lucas—see: Wyndham, John, 1903-1969.	
Parkhurst, Jane.	none
Parnov, Eremei IUdovich, 1935-	PG3485.A72
Parrish, Barney—see: Wolk, George.	
Parry, Michel.	none
Parvin, Brian.	none
Pascal, Jacques.	none
Pasnak, William.	none
Patchett, Mary E. (Mary Elwyn), 1897-	none
Paton, John.	none
Paton Walsh, Jill, 1937-	PR6066.A85
Patton, Chris.	none
Patton, Leah.	none
Paul, Barbara, 1931-	PS3566.A82615
Paulsen, Gary.	PS3566.A837
Paxson, Diana L.	none
Payne, Bernal C.	none
Payne, Robert, 1911-	PR6031.A93

Peacock, Thomas Love, 1785-1866.	PR5160-5164
Peake, Mervyn Laurence, 1911-1968.	PR6031.E183
Pearce, Barbara.	none
Pearl, Jack.	PS3566.E218
Pearlman, Gilbert.	none
Pearson, Edward.	none
Peck, Richard E.	PS3566.E253
Pedler, Kit.	PR6066.E35
Peel, Colin D.	PR6066.E36
Pemberton, Alan.	PR6066.E487
Pemberton, Max, Sir, 1863-1950.	PR6031.E4
Pemberton, Victor.	none
Pendleton, Don.	none
Pendray, G. Edward (George Edward), 1901-	PS3531.E4226
Penny, David G.	none
Pepper, Frank S.	none
Percy, Walker, 1916-	PS3566.E6912 [Z8672.59]
Perdue, Lewis.	PS3566.E69122
Pereira, W. D. (Wilfred Dennis), 1921-	PR6066.E65
Perkins, Michael.	none
Perkins, Sheldon.	none
Perry, Mark C.	none
Perry, Richard, 1944-	PS3566.E715
Perry, Roger.	none
Perry, Steve.	none
Pešek, Ludek.	PT2676.E74
Petaja, Emil, 1915-	PS3566.E745
Peters, David, 1927-	PR9390.9.P4
Peters, Elizabeth.	PS3563.E747
Peters, L. T.	PS3566.L7556
Peterson, John Victor.	none
Pettersson, Alan Rune.	none
Petty, John.	none
Petyo, Robert.	none
Peyton, Audrey.	none
Pfefferle, Seth.	none
Pfeil, Donald J.	PS3566.F43
Phelps, Elizabeth Stuart—see: Trusta, H., 1815-1852.	
Phelps, Gilbert.	PR6066.H4
Phillifent, John T.	none
Phillips, Alexander Moore, 1907-	none
Phillips, Lyn.	none
Phillips, Mark.	none
Phillips, Rog.	none
Phillpotts, Eden, 1862-1960.	PR5177

Phipson, Joan.	[Z8684.5] none
Picano, Felice, 1944-	PS3566.I25
Pierce, Meredith Ann.	none
Pierce, Tamora.	none
Piercy, Marge.	PS3566.I4
Pike, Christopher.	none
Pincher, Chapman.	PR6066.I47
Pini, Richard.	none
Pini, Wendy.	PS3566.I524
Pinkwater, Daniel Manus, 1941-	none
Pintaro, John.	none
Piper, H. Beam.	PS3566.I58
Piserchia, Doris.	PS3566.I7
Plante, Edmund.	none
Platt, Charles.	PS3566.L285
Plowright, Teresa.	PR9199.3.P556
Plym, Donald Lester.	none
Plym, Thea Ann.	none
Poe, Edgar Allan, 1809-1849.	PS2600-2648 [Z8699]
Pohl, Frederik.	PS3566.O36
Pohle, Robert W., 1949-	none
Pohlman, Edward, 1933-	PS3566.O38
Polikarpus, Viido.	PS3566.O46
Pollack, Rachel.	none
Pons, Maurice.	PQ2631.O6443
Pope, Elizabeth Marie, 1917-	none
Pope, Gustavus W.	PS2649.P422
Popescu, Petru.	PR9170.R63.P6+ PC840.26.O57
Posnick, Paul.	none
Pothan, Kap, 1929-	none
Potocki, Jan, hrabia, 1761-1815.	PQ2019.P87 [Z8709.13]
Pouns, Brauna E.	none
Pournelle, J. E.—see: Pournelle, Jerry, 1933-	
Pournelle, Jerry, 1933-	PS3566.O815
Powe, Bruce.	PR9199.3.P65
Powers, J. L.—see: Glasby, John.	
Powers, Louise E.	none
Powers, Tim, 1952-	PS3566.O95
Powys, John Cowper, 1872-1963.	PR6031.O867 [Z8710.5]
Powys, Theodore Francis, 1875-1953.	PR6031.O873 [Z8710.6]

Poyer, D. C.—see: Poyer, David.	
Poyer, David.	PS3566.O978
Poyer, Joe.	PS3566.O98
Praed, Campbell, Mrs., 1851-1935.	PR5189.P6
Pragnell, Festus.	none
Prantera, Amanda.	PR6066.R325
Pratchell, Terry.	PR6066.R34
Pratt, Fletcher, 1897-1956.	PS3531.R23
Pratt, Theodore, 1901-	PS3531.R248
Preiss, Byron.	none
Prescot, Dray—see: Bulmer, Kenneth, 1921-	
Prest, Thomas Peckett.	PR5189.P95
Preuss, Paul, 1942-	PS3566.R416
Preussler, Otfried.	PT2676.R42
Price, E. Hoffmann.	PS3566.R465
Price, Roger, 1941-	none
Price, Susan.	none
Priest, Christopher.	PR6066.R55
Priestley, J. B. (John Boynton), 1894-	PR6031.R6 [Z8713.535]
Proctor, George W.	PS3566.R588
Pronzini, Bill.	PS3566.R67
Prose, Francine, 1947-	PS3566.R68
Prosser, Harold Lee, 1944-	none
Prutkov, Koz'ma.	PG3363 [Z8883.55]
Pruyn, Leonard.	none
Pseudoman, Akkad—see: Northrup, Edwin Fitch, 1866-	
Ptacek, Kathryn.	none
Puccetti, Roland.	PS3566.U25
Pullman, Philip, 1946-	PR6066.U44
Purdom, Tom.	none
Purtill, Richard L., 1931-	PS3566.U77
Putney, Susan K.	none
Queen, Ellery.	PS3533.U4
Quiller-Couch, Arthur Thomas, Sir, 1863-1944.	PR5194-5195
Quinn, Seabury, 1889-1969.	PS3533.U69
Quirino, Joe, 1930-	PR9550.9.Q5
Quirino, José A.—see: Quirino, Joe, 1930-	
Rabin, Jennifer.	none
Rackham, John.	none
Radcliffe, Ann Ward, 1764-1823.	PR5200-5204
Rae, Hugh C.	PR6068.A25
Ramirez, Alice—see: Arkham, Constance.	
Ramsay, Jay—see: Campbell, Ramsey, 1946-	
Ramuz, C. F. (Charles Ferdinand), 1878-1947.	PQ2635.A35

	[Z8732.81]
Rand, Ayn.	PS3535.A547
Rand, Peter, 1940-	PS3568.A48
Randall, Bob.	PS3568.A489
Randall, Florence Engel, 1917-	PS3568.A493
Randall, Marta.	PS3568.A4964
Randall, Neil.	none
Randall, Robert, pseud.	PS3568.A497
Randisi, Robert J.	PS3568.A53
Randle, Kevin D.	none
Randolph, Arabella—see: Younger, Jack.	
Random, Alex—see: Rowland, Donald S.	
Rankine, John—see: Mason, Douglas R.	
Ransom, Bill.	none
Ranzetta, Luan.	none
Raphael, Rick.	PS3568.A614
Raspail, Jean.	PQ2635.A379
Raspe, Rudolf Erich, 1737-1794.	PT2452.R4
Rathjen, Carl Henry.	none
Rauch, Earl Mac, 1949-	PS3568.A79
Raucher, Herman.	PS3568.A8
Raven, Simon, 1927-	PR6068.A9
Ravenswood, Fritzen.	none
Ray, David, 1932-	PS3568.A9
Ray, N. L.	none
Ray, Rene.	none
Ray, Robert.	none
Ray, Trevor.	none
Rayer, Francis G.	none
Rayner, Claire.	PR6068.A949
Reade, Quinn.	none
Reamy, Tom.	PS3568.E25
Reaves, Michael.	PS3568.E269
Reed, Clifford C.	none
Reed, Dana.	none
Reed, David V.	none
Reed, Kit.	PS3568.E367
Reed, Robert.	none
Rees, Simon.	none
Reeve, Arthur Benjamin, 1880-1936.	PS3535.E354
Reeves, James.	PR6035.E38
Reeves, L. P.	none
Reginald, R.	PS3568.E4754
	[Z8736.47]
Reichert, Mickey Zucker.	none
Reinius, Trish, 1936-	PS3568.E4927

Reinsmith, Richard.	none
Reiss, Marc.	none
Relling, William.	none
Renard, Joseph.	none
Repp, Edward Earl, 1900-	none
Resnick, Michael D.	none
Reynolds, Alfred.	none
Reynolds, Bonnie Jones.	PS3568.E887
Reynolds, George W. M. (George William MacArthur), 1814-1879.	PR5221.R35
Reynolds, Mack.	PS3568.E895 [Z8740.9853]
Reynolds, Pamela.	none
Rheingold, Howard.	none
Rhinehart, Luke.	PS3568.H5
Rhodes, W. H. (William Henry), 1822-1876.	PS2698.R43
Rhys, Jack.	none
Ribeiro, Stella Carr.	none
Ricci, Barbara Guignon.	PS3568.I25
Rice, Anne, 1941-	PS3568.I265
Rice, Jeff.	none
Richards, Henry—see: Morrissey, Joseph Laurence, 1905-	
Richards, Joel.	none
Richards, Tony.	none
Richardson, Linda.	none
Richardson, Robert S. (Robert Shirley), 1902-	none
Richmond, Leigh.	none
Richmond, Walt.	none
Riddell, J. H., Mrs., 1832-1906.	PR5227.R33
Riding, Julia.	none
Rienow, Laura Train.	none
Rienow, Robert, 1907-	none
Rikhye, Ravi, 1944-	none
Rimmer, Robert H., 1917-	PS3568.I4
Ringel, Harry.	none
Rivere, Alec—see: Nuetzel, Charles.	
Rivkin, J. F.	none
Robbe-Grillet, Alain, 1922-	PQ2635.O117 [Z8747.67]
Robbins, David.	none
Robbins, Tom.	PS3568.O233
Robbins, Trina.	PS3568.O2334
Roberson, Jennifer, 1953-	PS3568.O236
Roberts, Arthur.	none
Roberts, James Hall—see: Duncan, Robert Lipscomb, 1927-	
Roberts, Jane, 1929-	PS3568.O2387

Roberts, Janet Louise, 1925-1982.	PS3552.R656
Roberts, John Maddox.	PS3568.O23874
Roberts, Keith, 1935-	PR6068.O15
Roberts, Lionel—see: Fanthorpe, R. Lionel.	
Roberts, Peter, 1950-	none
Roberts, Richard, 1941-	PS3568.O2473
Roberts, Willo Davis.	PS3568.O2478
Robertson, J. R.	none
Robertson, John.	none
Robeson, Kenneth.	none
Robinett, Stephen.	PS3568.O274
Robinson, Eleanor.	none
Robinson, Frank M.	PS3568.O2888
Robinson, Frank S.	none
Robinson, Jeanne.	none
Robinson, Kim Stanley.	PS3568.O2893
Robinson, Logan.	PS3568.O31224
Robinson, Philip Bedford, 1926-	PR6035.O573
Robinson, Spider.	PS3568.O3156
Robson, Michael.	none
Rocklynne, Ross.	none
Rockwood, Roy.	none
Roddenberry, Gene.	PS3568.O3424
Rodgers, Mary.	none
Rogers, Barbara, 1935-	PS3568.O39
Rogers, Mark E. (Mark Earl), 1952-	PS3568.O449
Rogers, Michael, 1950-	PS3568.O453
Rohan, Michael Scott.	PR6068.O354
Rohan, Mike Scott—see: Rohan, Michael Scott.	
Rohmer, Richard H.	PR9199.3.R58
Rohmer, Sax, 1883-1959.	PS3545.A653 [Z8949.27]
Roland, Howell.	none
Rolfe, Frederick, 1860-1913.	PR5236.R27 [Z8756.7]
Rolls, Brian.	none
Romano, Deane.	PS3568.O547
Romero, George A.	PS3568.O564
Romine, Aden Foster.	none
Romine, Mary Cox.	none
Ronald, Bruce W.	none
Rooke, Leon.	PS3568.O6
Roscoe, Theodore.	PS3535.O6423
Rose, Lawrence F.—see: Fearn, John Russell, 1908-1960.	
Rosenberg, Joel.	PS3568.O786
Roshwald, Mordecai, 1921-	none

Rosny, J. H., 1856-1940.	PQ2635.O56
Ross, Barnaby—see: Queen, Ellery.	
Ross, Clarissa—see: Ross, W. E. D. (William Edward Daniel), 1912-	
Ross, Marilyn—see: Ross, W. E. D. (William Edward Daniel), 1912-	
Ross, W. E. D. (William Edward Daniel), 1912-	PR9199.3.R5996
Rossiter, Oscar.	PS3568.O8475
Rossmann, John F.	none
Rossow, William Brigance, 1947-	none
Roszak, Theodore, 1933-	PS3568.O8495
Roth, Arthur J., 1925-	PS3568.O852
Roth, Philip.	PS3568.O855 [Z8761.2]
Rothberg, Abraham.	PS3568.O857
Rothman, Chuck.	none
Rothman, Milton.	none
Rothman, Tony.	none
Rotsler, William.	PS3568.O873
Rouch, James.	none
Rousseau, Victor—see: Emanuel, Victor Rousseau, 1879-	
Rovin, Jeff.	PS3568.O8884
Rowland, Donald S.	none
Rowley, Christopher B.	none
Roy, Archie.	none
Royal, Brian James.	PS3568.O96
Ruben, William S.	none
Rubens, Bernice.	PR6068.U2
Ruck, Berta, 1878-	PR6035.U3
Rucker, Rudy v. B. (Rudy von Bitter), 1946-	PS3568.U298
Rudhyar, Dane, 1895-	PS3535.U235
Rudorff, Raymond.	PR6068.U3
Ruemmler, John David.	none
Ruhen, Carl.	none
Rule, Ann.	PS3568.U42
Rundle, Anne.	PR6068.U7
Runyon, Charles W., 1928-	PS3568.U53
Ruse, Gary Alan, 1946-	PS3568.U72
Rush, Allison.	none
Rushdie, Salman.	PR9499.3.R8
Rusoff, Garry.	none
Russ, Joanna, 1937-	PS3568.U763
Russell, Bertrand, 1872-1970.	PR6035.U63 [Z8765.48]
Russell, Eric Frank, 1905-	PR6035.U66
Russell, John—see: Fearn, John Russell, 1908-1960.	
Russell, John Robert.	none
Russell, Ray.	PS3568.U77

Russell, William Clark, 1844-1911.	PR5280-5283
Russen, David, fl. 1705.	PR3671.R63
Russo, John, 1939-	none
Rutherford, Brett.	PS3568.U817
Rutherford, Edward.	PR6068.U88
Rutherford, Michael (Michael Andrew)	PS3568.U819
Ruuth, Marianne.	none
Ryan, Alan, 1943-	PS3568.Y26
Ryan, Thomas J. (Thomas Joseph), 1934-	PS3568.Y394
Ryder, James.	none
Ryman, Geoff.	none
Ryman, Ras.	none
Rypel, T. C.	none
Saberhagen, Fred, 1930-	PS3569.A215
Sacranie, Raj.	none
Sadler, Barry, 1940-	PS3569.A24
Saffron, Robert.	PS3569.A282
Sagan, Carl, 1934-	PS3569.A287
Sagnier, Thierry J.	none
Saint, H. F. (Harry F.)	PS3569.A38
Saki, 1870-1916.	PR6025.U675
Sallaska, Georgia.	PS3569.A46
Sallis, James, 1944-	PS3569.A469
Salmonson, Jessica Amanda.	none
Salsitz, R. A. V.—see: Vilott, Rhondi.	
Sambrot, William.	none
Sampson, Fay.	none
San Souci, Robert P.	none
Sanborn, Robin.	none
Sanders, Lawrence, 1920-	PS3569.A5125
Sanders, Scott R. (Scott Russell), 1945-	PS3569.A5137
Sangster, Jimmy.	PR6069.A53
Saperstein, David.	PS3569.A584
Sapir, Richard.	PS3569.A59
Sarabande, William.	none
Sarac, Roger—see: Caras, Roger A.	
Saralegui, Jorge.	none
Sarban—see: Wall, John W.	
Sargent, Craig.	none
Sargent, H. B.	none
Sargent, Pamela.	PS3569.A6887
Sargent, Sarah.	none
Sarrantonio, Al.	PS3569.A73
Sarton, May, 1912-	PS3537.A832
Saul, George Brandon, 1901-	PS3537.A866
Saul, John.	PS3569.A787

Saunders, Charles R.	none
Saunders, G. K.	none
Saunders, Jake.	none
Savage, Richard.	none
Savarin, Julian Jay.	PR6069.A937
Savchenko, Vladimir Ivanovich, 1933-	PG3485.8.V35
Savile, Frank Mackenzie.	PS3537.A9323
Savory, Gerald.	none
Savory, Teo.	PS3569.A85
Saward, Eric.	none
Sawde, Derek.	none
Saxon, Peter.	none
Saxon, Richard—see: Morrissey, Joseph Laurence, 1905-	
Saxton, Josephine.	PR6069.A96
Saxton, Mark.	PS3537.A979
Scanlon, Noel.	PR6069.C33
Scarborough, Elizabeth.	none
Schachner, Nathan, 1895-1955.	none
Schaffer, Gene.	none
Scheer, K. H.	none
Schenck, Hilbert, 1926-	none
Schlee, Ann.	PR6069.C514
Schmidt, Arno, 1914-	PT2638.M453
Schmidt, Dennis.	none
Schmidt, Stanley.	PS3569.C5158
Schmitz, James H., 1911-	PS3569.C5175
Schoell, William.	none
Scholz, Carter.	none
Schoonover, Lawrence L.	PS3569.C527
Schoonover, Shirley.	PS3569.C528
Schorer, Mark, 1908-	PS3537.C597
Schreiber, Harvey K.	none
Schulman, J. Neil (Joseph Neil), 1953-	PS3569.C539
Schutz, J. W.	none
Schwartz, Alan.	PS3569.C5648
Schwarz-Bart, Simone.	PQ2679.C43
Schweitzer, Darrell, 1952-	PS3569.C5684
Schwerin, Doris.	PS3569.C5697
Scliar, Moacyr.	PQ9698.29.C54
Scortia, Thomas N., 1926-	PS3569.C587
Scott, Alan.	none
Scott, Bill—see: Scott, William Neville.	
Scott, Jody.	none
Scott, Melissa.	none
Scott, Michael.	none
Scott Moncrieff, David.	none

Scott, Peg O'Neill.	none
Scott, Peter T.	none
Scott, William Neville.	PR9619.3.S4
Seaborn, Adam—see: Symmes, John Cleve, 1780-1829.	
Seare, Nicholas.	PS3569.E1763
Searls, Hank, 1922-	PS3569.E18
See, Carolyn.	PS3569.E33
Segraves, Kelly L.	PS3569.E45
Seignolle, Claude.	PQ2637.E39
Selden, George, 1929-	none
Sellers, Con.	PS3569.E575
Sellers, Mary.	none
Sellier, Charles E.	none
Sellings, Arthur, 1921-	PR6069.E37
Seltzer, David.	none
Seltzer, Richard.	PS3569.E584
Senn, Steve.	none
Serling, Rod, 1924-	PS3537.E654
Serrano, Miguel, 1917-	PQ8097.S57
Service, Pamela F.	none
Service, Robert W. (Robert William), 1874-1958.	PR6037.E72
Serviss, Garrett Putnam, 1851-1929.	PS3537.E68
Setlowe, Richard.	PS3569.E78
Seton, Anya.	PS3537.E787
Severance, Felix—see: Laumer, March.	
Severn, David, 1918-	none
Seymour, Alan.	PR6069.E72
Shaara, Michael.	PS3569.H2
Shackleford, Jack D.	none
Shackleton-Hill, Angela.	none
Shadbolt, Maurice.	PR9639.3.S5
Shaffer, A. (Anthony), 1926-	PR6069.H258
Shaffer, Eugene Carl.	none
Shannon, Doris.	PR9199.3.S5277
Shapiro, Neil.	none
Shapiro, Stanley.	PS3569.H3416
Sharman, Nick.	none
Sharp, William, 1855-1905.	PR5350-5358
Shaver, Richard S.	none
Shaw, Bob.	PR6069.H364
Shaw, Frederick L.	none
Shea, Michael, 1946-	PS3569.H39117
Shea, Robert.	PS3569.H39125
Shear, David.	PS3569.H3913
Shearing, Joseph—see: Bowen, Marjorie, pseud.	
Sheckley, Robert, 1928-	PS3569.H392

Shedley, Ethan I.	PS3569.H39214
Sheehan, Perley Poore, 1875-1943.	none
Sheffield, Charles.	PS3569.H39253
Shefner, Vadim Sergeevich, 1915-	PG3476.S466
Sheldon, Lee—see: Lee, Wayne C.	
Sheldon, Roy.	none
Sheldon-Williams, Miles.	PR6037.H426
Shelley, Mary Wollstonecraft, 1797-1851.	PR5397-5398 [Z8814.95]
Shelton, William Roy.	PS3569.H3937
Shepard, Lucius.	PS3569.H3939
Sherburne, Zoe.	none
Sherman, Harold Morrow, 1898-	PS3537.H763
Sherman, Jory.	PS3569.H43
Sherred, T. L.	PS3569.H4345
Sherrell, Carl.	none
Sherriff, R. C. (Robert Cedric), 1896-1975.	PR6037.H513
Shetterly, Will.	none
Shiel, M. P. (Matthew Phipps), 1865-1947.	PR6037.H524 [Z8816.9]
Shiner, Lewis.	none
Shiras, Wilmar H.	none
Shirley, John, 1953-	PS3569.H558
Shirley, Robert.	none
Shirreffs, Gordon D.	PS3569.H562
Shobin, David.	PS3569.H567
Shock, Julian—see: Williamson, J. N.	
Short, Jackson.	none
Shorter, Philip.	none
Shubin, Seymour.	PS3569.H754
Shulman, Sandra.	PS3569.H775
Shupp, Mike.	none
Shute, Nevil, 1899-1960.	PR6027.O54
Shwartz, Susan.	none
Siddons, Anne Rivers.	PS3569.I28
Sidney, Kathleen M.	PS3569.I32
Sidney-Fryer, Donald, 1934-	PS3569.I34
Siegal, Barbara.	none
Siegal, Scott.	none
Siegel, Martin.	none
Siegel, Robert, 1939-	PS3569.I382
Sievert, J. (John)	none
Silas, A. E.	none
Silbersack, John.	none
Silent, William T.	PS3569.I42
Sillitoe, Alan.	PR6037.I55

Silverberg, Robert.	PS3569.I472
	[Z8819.I35]
Simak, Clifford D., 1904-	PS3537.I54
	[Z8819.I42]
Simmons, Dan.	PS3569.I47292
Simmons, Geoffrey S.	PS3569.I4732
Simons, Les.	none
Simpson, George E.	PS3569.I4895
Sims, D. N.	none
Sinclair, Andrew.	PR6069.I5
Sinclair, May.	PR6037.I73
Sinclair, Quinn.	none
Sinclair, Upton, 1878-1968.	PS3537.I85
Singer, Isaac Bashevis, 1904-	PJ5129.S49
	[Z8819.55]
Singer, Marilyn.	none
Singer, Rochelle—see: Singer, Shelley.	
Singer, Shelley.	PS3569.I565
Siodmak, Kurt, 1902-	PR6037.I775
Sirota, Mike.	none
Sitwell, Osbert, 1892-1969.	PR6037.I83
Skal, David J.	none
Skaldaspillir, Sigfriour.	none
Skinkle, Dorothy E.	none
Skipp, John.	none
Skolsky, Syd Cohen, 1917-	none
Sky, Kathleen.	none
Sladek, John Thomas.	PS3569.L25
Sladen, Douglas Brooke Wheelton, 1856-1947.	PR5453.S14
Slaten, Jeff.	none
Slater, Jim, 1929-	none
Slater, Philip Elliot.	PS3569.L263
Slator, Henry J.	none
Slaughter, Jean—see: Doty, Jean Slaughter, 1924-	
Slavitt, David R., 1935-	PS3569.L3
Sleator, William.	none
Sloane, Robert C.	PS3569.L594
Sloane, William Milligan, 1906-	PS3537.L59
Slobodkin, Louis, 1903-	PS3537.L63
Slonaker, Larry.	
Slonczewski, Joan.	PS3569.L69
Slote, Alfred.	none
Small, Austin J.	none
Smeds, Dave.	none
Smith, A. C.	none
Smith, A. C. H. (Anthony Charles H.), 1935-	PR6069.M42

Smith, Andrew.	none
Smith, Arthur D. Howden (Arthur Douglas Howden), 1887-1945.	none
Smith, Basil Alec.	none
Smith, Clark Ashton, 1893-1961.	PS3537.M335 [Z8820.4]
Smith, Cordwainer, 1913-1966.	PS3523.I629
Smith, D. Alexander (David Alexander)	none
Smith, David C.	none
Smith, E. E. (Edward Elmer), 1890-1965.	PS3537.M349
Smith, Evelyn E.	PS3569.M53515
Smith, Garret.	none
Smith, George Henry, 1922-	none
Smith, George Oliver, 1911-	PS3537.M4478
Smith, Gregory Blake.	PS3569.M5356
Smith, Gregory J. (Gregory Jon)	PS3569.M5357
Smith, Guy N.	none
Smith, Kay Nolte.	PS3569.M537554
Smith, L. Neil.	none
Smith, Martin Cruz, 1942-	PS3569.M5377
Smith, Perry Michael, 1937-	PS3569.M5379
Smith, Phil.	none
Smith, Robert, 1920-	none
Smith, Robert Arthur.	none
Smith, Robert Charles.	PR6069.M53
Smith, Stephanie A.	PS3569.M5379777
Smith, Susan.	none
Smith, Thorne, 1893-1934.	PS3537.M835
Smith, W. J.	none
Smoodin, Roberta, 1952-	PS3569.M647
Sno, William.	none
Snodgrass, Melinda M., 1951-	none
Snyder, Cecil.	none
Snyder, Eugene V.	none
Snyder, Gene.	none
Snyder, Guy.	none
Snyder, Zilpha Keatley.	PS3569.N97
Sobel, Robert, 1931 Feb. 19-	none
Sobol, Donald J., 1924-	none
Sohl, Jerry.	PS3569.O4
Sommer-Bodenburg, Angela.	none
Somtow, S. P.—see: Sucharitkul, Somtow.	
Sonders, Mark.	none
Sørensen, Villy, 1929-	PT8175.S648
Sosna, Sharon.	none
Southall, Ivan.	PR9619.3.S6
Southesk, James Carnegie, Earl of, 1827-1905.	PR5459.S69

Souza, Steven M.	none
Sowden, Lewis.	PR6037.O85
Sparrow, Susanna.	none
Spector, Craig.	none
Spedding, A.	none
Spencer, Scott.	PS3569.P455
Sperry, Ralph A.	none
Spielberg, Steven, 1947-	PS3569.P493 [Z8830.89]
Spielman, Brenda Gates.	none
Spinrad, Norman.	PS3569.P55
Sprechman, J. R.	PS3569.P675
Springer, Nancy.	PS3569.P685
Spruill, Steven G.	PS3569.P733
St. Clair, Margaret.	PS3569.T118
St. George, E. A. (Elizabeth Ann), 1937-	none
St. George, Judith, 1931-	none
St. John, Philip—see: Del Rey, Lester, 1915-	
St. John, Wylly Folk.	none
Stableford, Brian M.	PR6069.T17
Stables, Gordon, 1840-1910.	none
Stacy, Ryder.	none
Stahl, Ben, 1910-	none
Stair, Bill, 1938-	none
Stallman, Robert.	none
Stamey, Sara.	none
Stanbury, C. M.	PS3569.T3315
Stanley, John, 1940-	none
Stanley, John (John B.)	PS3569.T3332
Stanwood, Brooks.	PS3569.T3342
Stapledon, Olaf, 1886-1950.	PR6037.T18 [Z8833.94]
Stapp, Robert.	PS3569.T3355
Stark, Raymond.	PS3537.T2422
Starr, Bill, 1944-	PS3569.T3362
Starr, Roland—see: Rowland, Donald S.	
Starrett, Vincent, 1886-1974.	PS3537.T246 [Z8834.2]
Stasheff, Christopher.	PS3569.T3363
Stashower, Daniel.	PS3569.T33635
Stateham, B. R.	none
Staton, Mary.	none
Statten, Vargo—see: Fearn, John Russell, 1908-1960.	
Steakley, John.	none
Steele, Addison E.—see: Lupoff, Richard A., 1935-	
Steele, Curtis.	PS3537.T2687

Steele, Daniel.	none
Steele, Linda.	none
Steele, Mary Q.	PS3569.T33843
Steen, Marguerite.	PR6037.T3
Steffanson, Con.	none
Steiger, Brad.	none
Stein, Benjamin, 1944-	PS3569.T36
Steinbeck, John, 1902-1968.	PS3537.T3234
Stephens, Brynne.	none
Stephens, James, 1882-1950.	PR6037.T4 [Z8841.84]
Stephenson, Andrew M.	none
Sterling, Bruce.	PS3569.T3876
Sterman, Betsy.	none
Sterman, Samuel.	none
Sternberg. Jacques.	PQ2637.T386
Steussy, Marti.	none
Stevens, Francis—see: Bennett, Gertrude Barrows, 1884-	
Stevenson, D. E. (Dorothy Emily), 1892-1973.	PR6037.T458
Stevenson, Florence.	PS3569.T455
Stevenson, Robert Louis, 1850-1894.	PR5480-5498 [Z8843]
Stevermer, C. J.	none
Stewart, Bruce.	PR6069.T4582
Stewart, Desmond, 1924-	PR6069.T4584
Stewart, Fred Mustard, 1932-	PS3569.T464
Stewart, George Rippey, 1895-	PS3537.T48545
Stewart, Mary, 1916-	PR6069.T46
Stewart, Ramona, 1922-	PS3569.T468
Stewart, Will—see: Williamson, Jack, 1908-	
Stickgold, Bob.	PS3569.T475
Stiegler, marc.	none
Stilson, Charles Billings.	none
Stine, G. Harry (George Harry), 1928-	none
Stine, H. William.	none
Stine, Hank.	none
Stine, Jovial Bob.	none
Stine, Megan.	none
Stine, R. L.	none
Stirling, S. M.	none
Stith, John E.	none
Stockbridge, Grant.	none
Stockton, Frank Richard, 1834-1902.	PS2925-2928 [Z8848]
Stoker, Bram, 1847-1912.	PR6037.T617 [Z8848.32]

Stolbov, Bruce.	PS3569.T6225
Stone, Alma.	PS3569.T629
Stone, Andy.	PS3569.T6293
Stone, Charlotte.	none
Stone, Elna.	PS3569.T633
Stone, Josephine Rector.	none
Stone, Leslie F.	none
Story, Jack Trevor.	PR6037.T7144
Stout, Rex, 1886-1975.	PS3537.T733 [Z8849.34]
Stout, Tim.	none
Stoutenberg, Adrien.	PS3569.T67
Stover, Leon E.	PS3569.T674
Stow, Randolph, 1935-	PR6037.T723 [Z8849.37]
Stratemeyer. Edward, 1862-1930.	PS3537.T817
Stratton, Chris.	none
Straub, Peter.	PS3569.T6914
Strauss, Victoria.	none
Streib, Dan.	none
Strete, Craig.	PS3569.T6935
Strickland, Brad.	none
Strieber, Whitley.	PS3569.T6955
Strike, Jeremy.	none
Strugatskii, Arkadii Natanovich.	PG3476.S78835
Strugatskii, Boris Natanovich.	none
Strutton, Bill.	none
Stryker, Hal—see: Smith, George Henry, 1922-	
Stuart, L. T.	none
Stuart, Sidney—see: Avallone, Michael.	
Stuart, W. J.—see: MacDonald, Philip.	
Sturgeon, Theodore.	PS3569.T875 [Z8852.32]
Sucharitkul, Somtow.	PS3569.U23
Sudak, Eunice.	none
Suddaby, Donald.	none
Sue, Eugène, 1804-1857.	PQ2446
Suffling, Mark.	none
Sugar, Andrew.	none
Sullivan, Faith.	PS3569.U3469
Sullivan, Mary W.	none
Sullivan, Mike.	none
Sullivan, Sheila.	PR6069.U3
Sullivan, Thomas.	none
Sullivan, Tim D.	PS3569.U3592
Sulzberger, C. L. (Cyrus Leo), 1912-	PS3569.U36

Summers, Dennis.	none
Susann, Jacqueline.	PS3569.U75
Sutcliff, Rosemary.	PR6037.U936 [Z8854.6]
Sutherland, James.	none
Sutphen, Van Tassel, 1861-1945.	PS3537.U946
Sutton, Henry—see: Slavitt, David R., 1935-	
Sutton, Jean.	none
Sutton, Jeff.	PS3569.U89
Sutton, Lee—see: Lee, Wayne C.	
Suyin, Han—see: Han, Suyin, pseud.	
Swain, Dwight V.	none
Swann, Brian.	PS3569.W256
Swann, Ingo, 1933-	none
Swann, Thomas Burnett.	PS3537.W3713
Swanwick, Michael.	PS3569.W28
Swearingen, Martha.	PS3569.W353
Swift, Jonathan, 1667-1745.	PR3720-3728 [Z8856]
Swigart, Rob.	PS3569.W52
Swycaffer, Jefferson P.	none
Sykes, Pamela, 1927-	PR6069.Y4
Sykes, S. C.	none
Symmes, John Cleve, 1780-1829.	PR5519.S45
Synge, Ursula, 1930-	none
Szerb, Antal, 1901-1945.	PH3351.S86 [Z8856.84]
Szilard, Leo.	none
Szydlow, Jarl—see: Vigliante, Mary.	
Tabler, Joseph.	none
Tabori, Paul, 1908-	PR6039.A15
Taine, John—see: Bell, Eric Temple, 1883-1960.	
Takei, George.	none
Talbot, Michael, 1953-	PR6070.A36
Tall, Stephen.	none
Talley, Steven.	none
Tannen, Mary.	PS3570.A54
Tarde, Gabriel de, 1843-1904.	none
Tarr, Judith.	PS3570.A655
Tarzan, Deloris Lehman.	none
Tate, Peter.	PR6070.A66
Taylor, Anna, 1944-	PR6070.A8
Taylor, Bernard, 1934-	PR6070.A884
Taylor, Charles D.	PS3570.A92723
Taylor, G. Jeffrey, 1944-	none
Taylor, Janelle.	none

Taylor, Keith.	none
Taylor, L. A. (Laurie Aylma), 1939-	PS3570.A943
Taylor, Ray Ward.	none
Taylor, Robert Lewis.	PS3539.A9654
Tedford, William G.	none
Telles, Lygia Fagundes.	PQ9697.T49
Tem, Steve Rasnic, 1950-	none
Temple, William F.	none
Tenn, William—see: Klass, Philip, 1920-	
Tennant, Emma.	PR6070.E52
Tepper, Sheri S.	none
Terman, Douglas, 1933-	PS3570.E676
Terts, Abram, 1925-	PG3476.S5414
Tessier, Thomas.	PR6070.E8
Tevis, Walter S.	PS3570.E95
Thacker, Eric.	PR6070.H3
Thanet, Neil—see: Fanthorpe, R. Lionel.	
Themerson, Stefan.	PR6039.H37
	PG7179.H4
Theobald, Robert.	PS3570.H37
Theroux, Paul.	PS3570.H4
Theydon, John.	none
Thiusen, Ismar—see: Macnie, John.	
Thoby-Marcelin, Philippe, 1904-1975.	PQ3949.T45
Thom, Robert, 1930-	PS3539.H5
Thomas, Chauncey.	none
Thomas, Craig.	PR6070.H56
Thomas, D. M.	PR6070.H58
Thomas, Dan.	none
Thomas, Donald.	PR6070.H6
Thomas, Elizabeth Marshall, 1931-	PS3570.H56253
Thomas, Martin.	none
Thomas, Ted.	PS3570.H59
Thompson, Allyn.	none
Thompson, Donald.	none
Thompson, Gene.	PS3570.H614
Thompson, Harlan.	none
Thompson, Howard.	none
Thompson, Joyce.	PS3570.H6414
Thompson, Julian F.	none
Thompson, Paul B.	none
Thompson, William Irwin.	PS3570.H645
Thorn, Joe.	PS3570.H648
Thornburg, Newton.	PS3570.H649
Thorne, Guy—see: Gull, Cyril Arthur Edward Ranger, 1876-1923.	
Thorne, Ian—see: May, Julian.	

Thorpe, Trebor—see: Fanthorpe, R. Lionel.	
Thurber, James, 1894-1961.	PS3539.H94 [Z8878.4]
Thurston, Robert.	PS3570.H86
Tierney, Richard L.	PS3570.I332
Tigges, John.	none
Tilley, Patrick.	PR6070.I38
Timlett, Peter Valentine.	none
Timlin, William M.	none
Timperley, Rosemary, 1920-	PR6070.I4
Tine, Robert.	PS3570.I48
Tiptree, James.	PS3570.I66
Titan, Earl—see: Fearn, John Russell, 1908-1960.	
Tobier, Arthur.	none
Todd, Ruthven, 1914-	PR6039.O26 [Z8883.15]
Tofte, Arthur.	PS3570.O424
Tolkien, J. R. R. (John Ronald Reuel), 1892-1973.	PR6039.O32 [Z8883.45]
Tolstoi, Aleksei Konstantinovich—see: Prutkov, Koz'ma.	
Tolstoy, Aleksey Nikolayevich, graf, 1883-1945.	PG3476.T6
Tomerlin, John, 1930-	none
Toombs, Jane.	PS3570.O55
Toomey, Robert E.	none
Topol, B. H.	none
Torro, Pel—see: Fanthorpe, R. Lionel.	
Townsend, John Rowe.	none
Tracy, Don, 1905-	PS3539.R124
Tracy, Louis, 1863-1928.	PS3539.R15
Train, Arthur Cheney, 1875-1945.	PS3539.R23
Tralins, Robert.	none
Transue, Jacob.	none
Travers, P. L. (Pamela L.), 1906-	none
Trebor, Robert.	none
Treece, Henry, 1911-1966.	PR6039.R38
Treibich, S. J.	none
Trell, Max.	PS3539.R374
Tremayne, Peter.	PR6070.R366
Treviño, Elizabeth Borton de, 1904-	PS3539.R455
Trevor, Elleston.	PR6039.R518
Trimble, Jacquelyn.	none
Trimble, Louis, 1917-	none
Trout, Kilgore—see: Farmer, Philip José.	
Trusta, H., 1815-1852.	PS3140-3143
Tryon, Thomas.	PS3570.R9
TSiolkovskii, K. (Konstantin), 1857-1935.	PG3470.T8

Tubb, E. C.	PR6070.U17
Tucker, James B.	PR6070.U26
Tucker, Wilson, 1914-	PS3539.U324
Tuleja, Thaddeus V.	none
Tullock, Joyce.	none
Tully, John, 1923-	none
Tuning, William.	none
Turman, John.	none
Turner, Frederick, 1943-	PS3570.U69
Turner, George.	PR6070.U717
Turner, James, 1909-1975.	PR6039.U64
Turney, Catherine.	PS3539.U865
Turtledove, Harry.	PS3570.U76
Turton, Godfrey Edmund.	PR6039.U75
Tutuola, Amos.	PR9387.9.T8
Tuttle, Lisa, 1952-	none
Twain, Mark, 1835-1910.	PS1300-1348
Tweed, Thomas Frederic.	none
Twitchell, Paul, 1908-1971.	PS3539.W58
Tyers, Kathy.	none
Tyler, Theodore.	none
Updike, John.	PS3571.P4 [Z8913.85]
Upton, Mark.	PS3571.P47
Urick, Kevin.	PS3571.R4
Uspenskii, P. D. (Petr Demianovich), 1878-1947.	PG3476.U675
Utley, Brian R.	none
Uttley, Alison, 1884-	PR6041.T8
Val Baker, Denys, 1917-	PR6072.A4
Vale, Rena Marie, 1898-	none
Vallejo, Doris.	PS3572.A413
Van Arnam, Dave.	none
Van Ash, Cay.	PR6072.A55
Van Doren, Mark, 1894-1972.	PS3543.A557
Van Dyke, Henry, 1852-1933.	PS3115-3118
Van Greenaway, Peter, 1929-	PR6072.A65
Van Herck, Paul—see: Herck, Paul van.	
Van Hise, Della.	none
Van Lhin, Erik—see: Del Rey, Lester, 1915-	
Van Loden, Erle.	none
Van Loon, Hendrik Willem, 1882-1944.	PS3543.A58
Van Rjndt, Philippe, 1950-	PR9199.3.V36
Van Scyoc, Sydney J.	PS3572.A4166
Van Sickle, Dirck.	PS3572.A539
Van Vogt, A. E. (Alfred Elton), 1912-	PS3543.A6546
Vance, Emily.	none

Vance, Jack, 1916-	PS3572.A424
Vance, Steve.	none
Vane, Sutton, 1888-	PR6043.A5
Vardeman, Robert E.	PS3572.A714
Varley, John, 1947-	PS3572.A724
Veley, Charles, 1943-	PS3572.E4
Venables, Hubert.	PS3572.E46
Venters, Archie.	none
Vercors, 1902-	PQ2603.R924
Verde, Campo—see: Greenfield, Irving A.	
Vernam, Glenn R.	PS3572.E75
Verne, Jules, 1828-1905.	PQ2469 [Z8934]
Vernon, Roger Lee, 1924-	none
Verrill, A. Hyatt (Alpheus Hyatt), 1871-1954.	none
Verseau, Dominique.	none
Viard, Henri, 1912-	PQ2682.I2
Victor, Steve.	none
Vidal, Gore, 1925-	PS3543.I26 [Z8942.19]
Viereck, George Sylvester, 1884-1962.	PS3543.I32
Vigliante, Mary.	none
Villiers de L'Isle Adam, Auguste, comte de, 1838-1889.	PQ2476.V4
Vilott, Rhondi.	none
Vilott-Salsitz, R. A. V.—see: Vilott, Rhondi.	
Vincent, Harl.	none
Vinge, Joan D.	PS3572.I53
Vinge, Vernor.	PS3572.I534
Vinicoff, Eric.	none
Vinter, Michael.	none
Visiak, E. H. (Edward Harold)	PR6043.I7
Vivian, Evelyn Charles H.	PR6043.I9
Vixen, Richard M.	PS3572.I87
Voight, Cynthia.	none
Voiskunskii, Evgenii, 1922-	PG3476.V622
Vollmann, William T.	PS3572.O395
Volsky, Paula.	none
Voltaire, 1694-1778.	PQ2070-2144 [Z8945]
Von Braun, Wernher, 1912-1977.	none
Von Niebelschütz, Wolf—see: Niebelschütz, Wolf von, 1913-1960.	
Vonnegut, Kurt.	PS3572.O5
Vorhies, John Royal.	none
Vyse, Michael.	none
Wade, Elizabeth.	none
Wade, Tom.	none

Wadey, Victor.	none
Wadsworth, Phyllis Marie.	none
Wagner, Geoffrey Atheling.	PS3545.A333
Wagner, Jack.	PS3573.A3863
Wagner, Karl Edward.	none
Wagner, Robin S.	none
Wagner, Sharon.	PS3573.A387
Waite, Arthur Edward, 1857-1942.	PR5706.W35 [Z8947.3]
Wakefield, Herbert Russell, 1889-	PR6045.A252
Walden, Mark.	none
Waldrop, Howard.	PS3573.A4228
Walker, David Harry, 1911-	PR9199.3.W33
Walker, Elizabeth.	none
Walker, Hugh.	none
Walker, Irma, 1921-	PS3573.A4253327
Walker, Robert W. (Robert Wayne), 1948-	none
Walker, Victoria, 1947-	none
Wall, John W.	PR6045.A3253
Wall, Mervyn, 1908-	PR6045.A3255
Wallace, David Foster.	PS3573.A425635
Wallace, Doreen Eileen Agnew, 1897-	PR6045.A3268
Wallace, Edgar, 1875-1932.	PR6045.A327
Wallace, Floyd L.	none
Wallace, Ian.	PS3573.A4258
Wallace, Irving, 1916-	PS3573.A426
Wallace, James.	none
Wallace, Pat.	none
Waller, Leslie, 1923-	PS3545.A565
Walling, William, 1926-	PS3573.A437
Wallis, Dave.	none
Wallis, G. McDonald.	none
Wallmann, Jeffrey M.	PS3573.A4395
Wallop, Douglass, 1920-	PS3573.A44
Walpole, Horace, 1717-1797.	PR3757.W2 [Z8947.9]
Walsh, J. M. (James Morgan), 1897-1952.	PR9619.3.W29
Walsh, Jill Paton—see: Paton Walsh, Jill, 1937-	
Walsh, Joan.	none
Walter, Elizabeth.	PR6073.A4285
Walter, William Grey, 1910-	none
Walters, Hugh.	PR6073.A44
Walters, R. R.	none
Walther, Daniel.	PQ2683.A454
Walton, Bryce, 1918-	none
Walton, Evangeline.	PS3545.A6296

Walton, Luke, 1941-	PS3573.A473
Walton, Stephen.	none
Walton, Su, 1944-	PR6073.A47
Wandrei, Donald, 1908-	PS3545.A643
Wandrei, Howard.	none
Wangerin, Walter.	PS3573.A477
Warburg, Sandol Stoddard.	none
Ward, Don.	none
Ward, Henry—see: Viard, Henri, 1912-	
Warner, Douglas.	PR6073.A723
Warner, Michael.	none
Warner, R. D.	none
Warner, Rex, 1905-	PR6045.A78
Warner, Sylvia Townsend, 1893-	PR6045.A812
Warner-Crozetti, R.	none
Warren, George, 1934-	PS3573.A773
Warren, William E., 1941-	none
Warrington, Freda.	none
Wartofsky, Victor.	PS3573.A783
Washburn, Mark.	PS3573.A788
Waterfield, Robin.	none
Waterloo, Stanley, 1846-1913.	PS3157.W318
Waters, T. A.	PS3573.A82
Watkin, Lawrence Edward, 1901-	PS3545.A8247
Watkins, Peter, 1934-	none
Watkins, William Jon.	PS3573.A845
Watson, Ian, 1943-	PR6073.A863
Watson, Jane Werner, 1915-	none
Watson, Patrick, 1929-	PR9199.3.W376
Watt-Evans, Lawrence, 1954-	PS3573.A859
Waugh, Evelyn, 1903-1966.	PR6045.A97 [Z8953.5]
Waugh, Harriet, 1944-	PR6073.A916
Wayman, Tony Russell.	none
Weaver, Lydia.	none
Weaver, Michael D.	PS3573.E179
Webb, Christopher—see: Wibberley, Leonard, 1915-	
Webb, Jean Francis.	PS3545.E322
Webb, Lucas.	PS3568.E4754
Webb, Sharon.	PS3573.E212
Webb, William Thomas.	none
Webster, Frederick Annesley Michael, 1886-	none
Webster, Joanne.	none
Webster, Josh.	none
Webster, Lyn.	none
Wedgelock, Colin.	none

Weekley, Ian.	PR6073.E24
Weeks, Stephen.	none
Wein, Len.	none
Weinbaum, Stanley Grauman, 1902-1935.	PS3545.E4636
Weinberg, George H.	PS3573.E3916
Weiner, Andrew, 1949-	PR9199.3.W398
Weiner, Ellis.	none
Weiner, Homer.	PS3573.E39327
Weinstein, Howard.	PS3573.E3965
Weinstein, Sol.	PS3573.E397
Weis, Margaret.	PS3573.E3978
Weisbecker, A. C. (Alan C.)	PS3573.E3979
Weiser, Melvin.	none
Welby, Philip.	none
Weldrick, Valerie.	none
Welfare, Mary.	none
Wellen, Edward.	none
Welling, Lois.	none
Wellman, Manly Wade, 1905-	PS3545.E52858
Wells, Basil, 1912-	none
Wells, H. G. (Herbert George), 1866-1946.	PR5770-5778 [Z8964.8]
Wells, Robert.	none
Wells, William K.	none
Wendorf, Patricia.	PR6073.E49
Werfel, Franz, 1890-1945.	PT2647.E77
Wernick, Saul.	none
Werper, Barton.	none
Wesley, Mary.	PR6073.E753
Wessex, Martyn.	none
West, Anthony, 1914-	PR6073.E763
West, Carl.	none
West, Jessamyn.	PS3545.E8315
West, Lindsay.	none
West, Nathanael, 1903-1940.	PS3545.E8334 [Z8968.38]
West, Owen—see: Koontz, Dean R. (Dean Ray), 1945-	
West, Rebecca, Dame, 1892-	PR6045.E8 [Z8968.4]
West, Wallace.	none
Westall, Robert.	none
Westerman, Percy Francis, 1876-1959.	none
Westheimer, David.	PS3573.E88
Westlake, Donald E.	PS3573.E9
Weston, Carolyn.	PS3573.E92
Weston, George, 1880-	none

Weston, Susan.	PS3573.E9243
Wetanson, Burt.	PS3573.E9247
Wetherell, June.	PS3545.E917
Weverka, Robert.	PS3573.E96
Weyrick, Becky Lee.	none
Wharton, Edith, 1862-1937.	PS3545.H16 [Z8969.2]
Wheatley, Dennis, 1897-	PR6045.H127 [Z8969.28]
Wheeler, J. Craig.	PS3573.H4325
Wheeler, Paul, 1934-	PR6073.H4
Wheeler, Scott.	none
Wheeler, Thomas Gerald.	none
Whitaker, David.	none
Whitby, Sharon.	none
White, Alan, 1924-	PR6073.H49
White, Alicen.	none
White, Edmund, 1940-	PS3573.H463
White, Edward Lucas, 1866-1934.	PS3545.H518
White, James, 1928-	PR6073.H494
White, Jane, 1934-	PR6073.H498
White, Jon Ewbank Manchip, 1924-	PR6073.H499
White, Mary Alice.	none
White, Stewart Edward, 1873-1946.	PS3545.H6
White, T. H. (Terence Hanbury), 1906-1964.	PR6045.H2 [Z8970.78]
White, Ted.	PS3573.H4749
Whiteford, Wynne.	none
Whitehead, Henry S.	none
Whiteson, Leon.	PR9199.3.W457
Whiting, Sydney, d. 1875.	PR5797.W54
Whitmore, Charles.	PS3573.H525
Whitten, Les, 1928-	PS3573.H566
Whittington, Henry.	none
Wibberley, Leonard, 1915-	PS3573.I2
Wicks, Mark.	PR6045.I347
Widener, Don.	PS3573.I27
Wiesel, Elie, 1928-	PQ2683.I32
Wilde, Oscar, 1854-1900.	PR5810-5828 [Z8975]
Wilder, Cherry.	none
Wilding, Philip.	none
Wilhelm, Kate.	PS3573.I434
Wilhelm, Lambert—see: Lambert, William J.	
Wilkes, Marilyn Z.	none
Wilkins, Mary E.—see: Freeman, Mary Eleanor Wilkins, 1852-1930.	

Wilkins, Vaughan, 1894-	none
Wilkinson, Vernon.	none
Willard, Nancy.	PS3573.I444
Willeford, Charles Ray, 1919-	PS3545.I464
Willer, Jim.	PR9199.3.W49
Willett, John, 1932-	none
William, Barry.	none
Williams, Charles, 1886-1945.	PR6045.I5 [Z8976.3]
Williams, Eric Cyril.	PR6073.I42586
Williams, Gordon M., 1934-	PR6073.I426
Williams, Jay, 1914-	PS3545.I528455
Williams, John Alfred, 1925-	PS3573.I4495
Williams, Kit.	PR6073.I43227
Williams, Mary.	PR6073.I4323
Williams, Michael Lindsay.	none
Williams, Nick Boddie.	none
Williams, Paul O., 1935-	PS3573.I45532
Williams, Robert Moore.	none
Williams, Roger.	none
Williams, T. Owen.	none
Williams, Tad.	none
Williams, Tennessee, 1911-	PS3545.I5365
Williams, Ursula Moray, 1911-	PR6045.I5462
Williams, Walter Jon.	PS3573.I456213
Williamson, Chet.	none
Williamson, George Hunt, 1926-	none
Williamson, J. N. (Jerry N.)	none
Williamson, Jack, 1908-	PS3545.I557 [Z8976.454]
Willis, Connie.	PS3573.I45652
Willis, Maud.	none
Wilson, Angus.	PR6045.I577 [Z8976.485]
Wilson, Colin, 1931-	PR6073.I44 [Z8976.487]
Wilson, F. Paul (Francis Paul)	PS3573.I45695
Wilson, Granville.	none
Wilson, Merzie.	none
Wilson, Richard, 1920-	none
Wilson, Robert Anton, 1932-	PS3573.I4662
Wilson, Robert Charles, 1951-	PS3573.I4663
Wilson, Robert Hendrie.	PR6073.I4738
Wilson, Snoo, 1948-	PR6073.I475
Wilson, Steve, 1943-	PR6073.I4752
Wiltshire, David.	none

Wind, David.	none
Windburn, Charles.	none
Winfield, Dick.	none
Wingrave, Anthony—see: Wright, Sydney Fowler, 1874-1967.	
Winski, Norman.	none
Winslow, Dorian—see: Winston, Daoma, 1922-	
Winslow, Pauline Glen.	PR6073.I553
Winsor, George McLeod.	PR6045.I723
Winston, Daoma, 1922-	PS3545.I7612
Winterbotham, Russell Robert, 1904-	none
Winterfeld, Henry.	PT2647.I723
Winters, Logan.	none
Winthrop, Elizabeth.	none
Wise, Arthur, 1923-	PR6073.I75
Wiseman, David.	none
Wisher, W. H.	none
Wisler, G. Clifton.	PS3573.I877
Wismer, Donald.	none
Wittig, Monique.	PQ2683.I8
Wobig, Ellen.	none
Wodehouse, P. G. (Pelham Grenville), 1881-1975.	PR6045.O53 [Z8979.5]
Wodhams, Jack.	none
Wold, Allen.	PS3573.O46
Wolf, Chris L.	none
Wolf, Gary K.	PS3573.O483
Wolfe, Aaron—see: Koontz, Dean R. (Dean Ray), 1945-	
Wolfe, Bernard, 1915-	PS3573.O49
Wolfe, Gene.	PS3573.O52
Wolfe, Louis.	none
Wolfman, Marv.	none
Wolitzer, Meg.	PS3573.O564
Wolk, George.	PS3573.O565
Wollheim, Donald A.	PS3573.O566
Womack, Jack.	PS3573.O575
Wood, Barbara.	PS3573.O5877
Wood, Bari, 1936-	PS3573.O588
Wood, Bridget.	none
Wood, Charles Erskine Scott, 1852-1944.	PS3545.O465
Wood, J. A.	none
Wood, Robert Williams, 1868-1955.	none
Woodard, Edwin.	none
Woodcott, Keith—see: Brunner, John, 1934-	
Woodhouse, Martin, 1932-	PR6073.O616
Woodley, Richard.	PS3573.O626
Woolf, Virginia, 1882-1941.	PR6045.O72

	[Z8984.2]
Woolfolk, William.	PS3573.O65
Woolley, Persia, 1935-	PS3573.O68
Woolrich, Cornell, 1903-1968.	PS3515.O6455
Wormser, Richard Edward, 1908-	PS3545.O88
Wouk, Herman, 1915-	PS3545.O98
Wrede, Patricia C.	none
Wren, M. K.	PS3573.R43
Wren, Thomas.	none
Wright, Austin Tappan, 1883-1931.	none
Wright, Glover.	PR6073.R488
Wright, Grahame, 1947-	PR6073.R49
Wright, Gregory Scott.	none
Wright, Guier S.	none
Wright, Kenneth—see: Del Rey, Lester, 1915-	
Wright, Lan.	none
Wright, Sydney Fowler, 1874-1967.	PR6045.R45
Wright, T. M., 1947-	PS3573.R544
Wrightson, Patricia.	none
Wu, William F.	none
Wul, Stefan.	PQ2683.U4
Wurlitzer, Rudolph.	PS3573.U7
Wurts, Janny.	none
Wylie, Elinor, 1885-1928.	PS3545.Y45
Wylie, Jonathan.	none
Wylie, Laura.	none
Wylie, Philip, 1902-1971.	PS3545.Y46
Wyndham, John, 1903-1969.	PR6045.Y64
Wynne, John.	PS3573.Y624
Xanthus, Xavier—see: Laumer, March.	
Yarbro, Chelsea Quinn, 1947-	PS3575.A7
Yates, Alan—see: Brown, Carter, 1923-	
Yates, W. R.	none
Yep, Laurence.	PS3575.E6
Yermakov, Nicholas.	none
Yolen, Jane.	PS3575.O43
York, Rebecca.	none
Yorke, Preston.	none
Young, Donna J.	PS3575.O783
Young, Jim.	none
Young, Robert—see: Payne, Robert, 1911-	
Young, Robert F.	PS3575.O84
Younger, Jack.	none
Yourcenar, Marguerite.	PQ2649.O8
Yuill, P. B.	PR6073.I426
Yulsman, Jerry.	PS3575.U4

Zacharia, Irwin.	none
Zachary, Hugh.	PS3576.A23
Zagat, Arthur Leo, 1896-1949.	none
Zahn, Timothy.	PS3576.A33
Zamiatin, Evgenii Ivanovich, 1884-1937.	PG3476.Z34 [Z8997.4]
Zarem, Lewis.	none
Zebrowski, George, 1945-	PS3576.E35 [Z8997.825]
Zeigfreid, Karl—see: Fanthorpe, R. Lionel.	
Zeigfried, Karl.	none
Zelazny, Roger.	PS3576.E43 [Z8997.829]
Zerwich, Chloe.	none
Zetford, Tully—see: Bulmer, Kenneth, 1921-	
Zezza, Carlo, 1936-	PS3576.E95
Zhuravleva, V. (Valentina)	none
Zierold, Norman J.	none
Zimmer, Paul Edwin.	none
Zimpel, Lloyd.	PS3576.I515
Zoss, Joel.	none
Zuk, Beverly C.	none

LC LITERATURE TABLES

In determining the cutters of individual literary works by one author, one must take into account certain numbers reserved for other purposes. A1-6 are reserved for collected works: A11-13 for collected works, A15 for collected fiction, A16 for collected essays, A17 for collected poems, A19 for collected plays, A6 for selected works (by date). A6 is the most commonly used of these "dump" numbers, often being used for omnibus collections of novels by one author (*e.g.*, a book called *Three novels* by Robert A. Heinlein might be classed in PS3515.E288A6 1987). The cutter stays the same for all books of this type, only the year of publication changing; if more than one title is published in the same year, they are differentiated by additional letters (*e.g.*, PS3515.E288A6 1987b). Similarly, Z459-999 is reserved for criticism (Z459 for dictionaries and indexes, Z46-479 for autobiographies, journals, and memoirs, Z48 for collections of letters, Z481-499 for letters to and from specific correspondents, and Z5-999 for general criticism (in alphabetical order by main entry). Because of these reserved numbers, literary works by one author beginning with the letters "A" and "Z" must be squeezed into A61-99 and Z11-458, respectively, and spread across the alphabet. Thus, the paperback edition of Peter Tremayne's *Zombie* might be classed in PR6070.R366Z37 1987, *not* in PR6070.R366Z65 1987 (Z65 being reserved for criticism). Moreover, AACR2's revised filing rules require that titles whose first words consist of numbers file *before* the letter "A"; thus, LC classed Richard Lamm's novel *1988* in PS3562.A4643A615, near the beginning of the "A" section reserved for individual titles (A61-99).

The national literature tables for authors are arranged by language, nationality, and period (usually a century or half-century), in that order, the authors being classed in each period in strict alphabetical order according to AACR2 filing rules. The major literatures (English, French, German, American, etc.), have two spans of numbers each reserved for twentieth-century authors, the demarcation line being 1960 (but in practice, often the 1950s). Smaller literatures may reserve one number for the entire twentieth century. The tables below provide detailed comparisons between the major literatures reflected in this manual.

AUTHOR NUMBERS BY NATIONALITY AND DATE

	19th cent.	1900-60	1961-
Afrikaans literature	PT6590 A-Z	PT6590 A-Z	PT6592-.36
American literature	PS991-3369	PS3500-49	PS3550-76
Argentine literature	PQ7797 A-Z	PQ7797 A-Z	PQ7798-.36
Bohemian literature	PG5038 A-Z	PG5038 A-Z	PG5039-.36
Brazilian literature	PQ9697 A-Z	PQ9697 A-Z	PQ9698-.36
Bulgarian literature	PG1037 A-Z	PG1037 A-Z	PG1038-.36
Chilean literature	PQ8097 A-Z	PQ8097 A-Z	PQ8098-.36
Columbian literature	PQ8179 A-Z	PQ8179 A-Z	PQ8180-.36
Cuban literature	PQ7389 A-Z	PQ7389 A-Z	PQ7390 A-Z
Danish literature	PT8100-8167	PT8175 A-Z	PT8176-.36
Dutch literature	PT5800-5880	PT5800-80	PT5881-.36
Ecuadorean literature	PQ8219 A-Z	PQ8219 A-Z	PQ8220-.36
English literature	PR3991-5925	PR6000-49	PR6050-76
Finnish literature	PH355 A-Z	PH355 A-Z	PH355 A-Z
French literature	PQ2149-2551	PQ2600-51	PQ2660-86
French Canadian lit.	PQ3919 A-Z	PQ3919 A-Z	PQ3919.2 A-Z
German literature	PT1799-2592	PT2600-53	PT2660-88*
Guatemalan literature	PQ7499 A-Z	PQ7499 A-Z	PQ7499.2 A-Z
Hungarian literature	PH3201-3381	PH3201-3381	PH3201-3381
Italian literature	PQ4675-4734	PQ4800-51	PQ4860-86
Japanese literature	PL800-820	PL821-843	PL844-866*
Mexican literature	PQ7297 A-7	PQ7297 A-Z	PQ7298-.36
Norwegian literature	PT8800-8942	PT8950 A-Z	PT8951-.36
Polish literature	PG7158 A-Z	PG7158 A-Z	PG7159-85
Romanian literature	PC839 A-Z	PC839 A-Z	PC840-.36
Russian literature	PG3450-3470	PG3476 A-Z	PG3477-90*
Spanish literature	PQ6500-6576	PQ6600-47	PQ6650-76
Swedish literature	PT9725-9850	PT9875 A-Z	PT9876-.36
Welsh literature	PB2298 A-Z	PB2298 A-Z	PB2298 A-Z
Yiddish literature	PJ5129 A-Z	PJ5129 A-Z	PJ5129 A-Z

*[German literature: 1700-1860/70; 1860/70-1960; 1961- ; Japanese literature: 1868-1926; 1926-1945; 1945- ; Russian literature: 1870-1917; 1917-1960; 1961- .]

TWENTIETH-CENTURY AUTHOR NUMBERS
BY INITIAL LETTER OF LAST NAME

Names	PS	PS	PR	PR	PQ	PQ	PT	PT	PT
A.	3501	3551	6001	6051	2601	2661	2601	2661	9876.1
B.	3503	3552	6003	6052	2603	2662	2603	2662	9876.12
C.	3505	3553	6005	6053	2605	2663	2605	2663	9876.13
D.	3507	3554	6007	6054	2607	2664	2607	2664	9876.14
E.	3509	3555	6009	6055	2609	2665	2609	2665	9876.15
F.	3511	3556	6011	6056	2611	2666	2611	2666	9876.16
G.	3513	3557	6013	6057	2613	2667	2613	2667	9876.17
H.	3515	3558	6015	6058	2615	2668	2615	2668	9876.18
I.	3517	3559	6017	6059	2617	2669	2617	2669	9876.19
J.	3519	3560	6019	6060	2619	2670	2619	2670	9876.2
K.	3521	3561	6021	6061	2621	2671	2621	2671	9876.21
L.	3523	3562	6023	6062	2623	2672	2623	2672	9876.22
M.	3525	3563	6025	6063	2625	2673	2625	2673	9876.23
N.	3527	3564	6027	6064	2627	2674	2627	2674	9876.24
O.	3529	3565	6029	6065	2629	2675	2629	2675	9876.25
P.	3531	3566	6031	6066	2631	2676	2631	2676	9876.26
Q.	3533	3567	6033	6067	2633	2677	2633	2677	9876.27
R.	3535	3568	6035	6068	2635	2678	2635	2678	9876.28
S.	3537	3569	6037	6069	2637	2679	*	*	9876.29
T.	3539	3570	6039	6070	2639	2680	2642	2682	9876.3
U.	3541	3571	6041	6071	2641	2681	2643	2683	9876.31
V.	3543	3572	6043	6072	2643	2682	2645	2684	9876.32
W.	3545	3573	6045	6073	2645	2683	2647	2685	9876.33
X.	3546	3574	6046	6074	2647	2684	2649	2686	9876.34
Y.	3547	3575	6047	6075	2649	2685	2651	2687	9876.35
Z.	3549	3576	6049	6076	2651	2686	2653	2688	9876.36

[*German authors whose last names begin with S: PT2637 (S-Scg), 2638 (Sch), 2639 (Sci-Sudd), 2640 (Sudermann, Hermann), 2641 (Sudf-Sz); PT2679 (Sa-Scg), 2680 (Sch), 2681 (Sci-Sz).]

OTHER ENGLISH LANGUAGE AUTHOR NUMBERS (A-Z)
(Authors writing in English)

PR9105.9	France.
PR9115.9	Greece.
PR9144.9	Norway.
PR9170.R63	Romania.
PR9199.2	Canada—19th century.
PR9199.3	Canada—20th century.
PR9265.9	Jamaica.
PR9369.3	South Africa—20th century.
PR9381.9	Kenya.
PR9387.9	Nigeria.
PR9390.9	Zimbabwe.
PR9399.9	Tanzania.
PR9402.9	Uganda.
PR9405.9	Zambia.
PR9440.9	Sri Lanka.
PR9499.3	India—20th century.
PR9510.9	Israel.
PR9550.9	Philippine Islands
PR9619.2	Australia—19th century.
PR9619.3	Australia—20th century.
PR9639.2	New Zealand—19th century.
PR9639.3	New Zealand—20th century.

IV
ARTIST MAIN ENTRIES
AND ARTIST NUMBERS

INTRODUCTION

Artist main entries are established in the same ways as author main entries, according to the rules established in AACR2. Artist numbers, however, are assigned not only by country and period, but by medium as well. Hence, it is not uncommon for an artist to have more than one number; prolific or versatile artists such as Picasso may have a half dozen or more, one for each field in which he has worked. Since artists are not normally assigned a number unless a portfolio, retrospective, or exhibition of his work has been published in book form and cataloged by the Library of Congress, only about half of the prominent SF artists have been assigned at least one number to date. In general, ND corresponds to painting, NC to illustration, N to general art, and PN to comic strips.

Achilleos, Chris, 1947-	NC978.5.A25
Asprin, Robert.	PN6727.A76
Austin, Alicia.	NC975.5.A9
Barlowe, Wayne Douglas.	NC975.5.B36
Barr, George, 1937-	NC975.5.B37
Bishofs, Maris.	NC1729.B57
Bodé, Vaughn, d. 1975.	NC975.5.B6
Bok, Hannes, 1914-1964.	none
Bonestell, Chesley.	ND2888.B66
Burns, Jim.	none
Cherry, David A.	N6737.C47
Chien-Eriksen, Nancy.	NC139.C52
D'Achille, Gino.	none
Dean, Martyn.	none
Dean, Roger, 1944-	N6537.D434
DiFate, Vincent.	N6537.D45
Dillon, Diane.	none
Dillon, Leo.	N6537.D475
Doran, Colleen, 1963-	PN6727.D67

Ellis, Dean.	none
Emshwiller, Ed.	none
Fabian, Stephen E., 1930-	NC975.5.F25
Finlay, Virgil.	NC975.5.F5
Fitzpatrick, Jim.	none
Foglio, Phil.	N6727.F64
Foss, Chris.	ND497.F64
Frazetta, Frank.	N6537.F75
	NC1850.F7
Freas, Frank Kelly, 1922-	N6537.F778
	NC975.5.F74
Froud, Brian.	NC978.5.F76
Gallardo Villaseñor, Gervasio, 1934-	ND813.G23
Gaughan, Jack.	none
Giger, H. R. (Hansreudi), 1940-	N7143.G48
Green, Michael, 1943-	NC975.5.G73
Hildebrandt, Greg.	NC975.5.H54
	N6537.H525
Hildebrandt, Tim.	none
Hill, Cathy.	none
Johnston, Joe.	NC975.5.J63
	NC139.J63
Jones, Peter A.	ND497.J626
Kaluta, Michael William.	none
Kirk, Tim.	NC975.5.K57
Krenkel, Roy G., 1918-	NC139.K73
Lee, Alan.	none
Lee, Elaine.	PN6728.L38
Lehr, Paul.	none
Maitz, Don.	none
McCall, Robert, 1919-	ND237.M4116
McQuarrie, Ralph.	none
Morrill, Rowena, 1944-	none
Morrow, Gray.	none
Nielsen, Palle, 1920-	NC275.N5
Nino, Alex.	none
Oakley, Graham.	none
Potter, J. K.	none
Powers, Richard.	none
Racle, Paul, 1932-	ND853.R25
Reynolds, Kay, 1951-	PN6727.R46
Reynolds, Mike, 1954-	none
Robbins, Trina.	none
Sale, Tim.	none
Salomoni, Tito.	none
Schoenherr, John.	none

Schomburg, Alec.	none
Sime, Sidney H.	NC978.5.S55
Siudmak, Wojtek, 1942-	NC989.P62.S58+
Steranko, James.	none
Sweet, Darrell.	none
Thole, Karel, 1914-	NC983.5.T4
Tolkien, J. R. R. (John Ronald Reuel), 1892-1973.	NC242.T65
Vallejo, Boris.	NC975.5.V34
	ND237.V14
Van Allsburg, Chris.	none
Van Dongen, H. R.	none
Waldron, Lamar, 1954-	PN6727.W27
Wenske, Helmut, 1940-	NC981.5.W46
Whelan, Michael, 1950-	NC975.5.W48
White, Tim, 1952-	ND498.W48
Wilks, Mike.	NC242.W56
Williams, Gilbert, 1950-	ND237.W7114
Williams, Kit.	N6797.W55
Wilson, Gahan.	NC1429.W5785
Woodroffe, Patrick, 1940-	N6797.W66
Wulfing, Sulamith, 1901-	ND1954.W78
Wyatt, Joan.	ND1942.W9

V
MOTION PICTURE MAIN ENTRIES AND CLASSIFICATION NUMBERS

INTRODUCTION

Books about individual motion pictures, or motion picture screenplays themselves, are classed in PN1997. Each film receives a unique cutter number derived from the first letter of the title; a second cutter for main entry completes the classification for a particular book. Relatively few science fiction movies have received individual numbers. The subject heading for each film is the motion picture title plus the appellation (Motion picture); these may be subdivided further as required. Films produced at different dates with the same title (remakes, for example) are identified by adding dates to the appellation—see the film *Dracula* below.

1984 (Motion picture)	none
2001: a space odyssey (Motion picture)	PN1997.T86
2010 (Motion picture)	PN1997.A2143
Alien (Motion picture)	PN1997.A32253
Aliens (Motion picture)	none
Andromeda strain (Motion picture)	none
Back to the future (Motion picture)	none
Barbarella (Motion picture)	none
Battlestar Galactica (Motion picture)	none
Black hole (Motion picture)	PN1997.B595
Blade runner (Motion picture)	none
Cabinet der Dr. Caligari (Motion picture)	PN1997.C18
Clockwork orange (Motion picture)	none
Close encounters of the third kind (Motion picture)	none
Creature from the black lagoon (Motion picture)	none
Dark crystal (Motion picture)	PN1997.D313353
Dark star (Motion picture)	none
Day the Earth stood still (Motion picture)	none
Destination Moon (Motion picture)	none
Dr. Jekyll and Mr. Hyde (Motion picture)	PN1997.D55
Dr. Strangelove (Motion picture)	none

Dracula (Motion picture : 1931)	none
Dune (Motion picture)	PN1997.D8473
E.T., the extra-terrestrial (Motion picture)	PN1997.E183
Empire strikes back (Motion picture)	PN1997.E624
Escape from New York (Motion picture)	none
Fahrenheit 451 (Motion picture)	none
Fantasia (Motion picture)	PN1997.F3317
Fantastic voyage (Motion picture)	none
Flash Gordon (Motion picture)	none
Fly (Motion picture)	none
Forbidden planet (Motion picture)	none
Frankenstein (Motion picture)	none
Ghostbusters (Motion picture)	PN1997.G4453
Great Muppet caper (Motion picture)	PN1997.G6873
Howard the duck (Motion picture)	none
Illustrated man (Motion picture)	none
Indiana Jones and the Temple of Doom (Motion picture)	PN1997.I513
Invasion of the body snatchers (Motion picture)	none
Invisible man (Motion picture)	none
King Kong (Motion picture : 1933)	PN1997.K437
King Kong (Motion picture : 1976)	PN1997.K4374
Krull (Motion picture)	none
Labyrinth (Motion picture)	none
Logan's run (Motion picture)	none
Lord of the rings (Motion picture)	PN1997.L725
Lost world (Motion picture)	none
Mad Max (Motion picture)	none
Mad Max beyond Thunderdome (Motion picture)	none
Man who fell to Earth (Motion picture)	none
Metropolis (Motion picture)	none
Muppet movie (Motion picture)	none
Night of the living dead (Motion picture)	PN1997.N5215
Nightmare on Elm Street (Motion picture)	PN1997.N5224
Nightmare on Elm Street II, Freddy's revenge (Motion picture)	none
Nightmare on Elm Street III (Motion picture)	none
Outland (Motion picture)	PN1997.O9
Planet of the apes (Motion picture)	none
Play it again, Sam (Motion picture)	PN1997.P5243
Popeye (Motion picture)	PN1997.P56
Quest for fire (Motion picture)	none
Raiders of the lost ark (Motion picture)	none
Return of the Jedi (Motion picture)	PN1997.R515
Road warrior (Motion picture)	none
Rocky horror picture show (Motion picture)	PN1997.R57547

Rollerball (Motion picture)	none
Silent running (Motion picture)	none
Sleeper (Motion picture)	none
Somewhere in time (Motion picture)	none
Spider-Man (Motion picture)	none
Star trek (Motion picture)	PN1997.S65932
Star trek II, the wrath of Khan (Motion picture)	PN1997.S65935
Star trek III, the search for Spock (Motion picture)	PN1997.S659363
Star trek IV, the voyage home (Motion picture)	PN1997.S659373
Star wars (Motion picture)	PN1997.S65943
Starman (Motion picture)	none
Superman (Motion picture)	PN1997.S853
Superman II (Motion picture)	none
Superman III (Motion picture)	none
Superman IV, the quest for peace (Motion picture)	none
Terminator (Motion picture)	none
Things to come (Motion picture)	none
THX 1138 (Motion picture)	none
Time after time (Motion picture)	none
Time machine (Motion picture)	none
Tron (Motion picture)	none
War of the worlds (Motion picture)	PN1997.W3363
Watership down (Motion picture)	PN1997.W343
Westworld (Motion picture)	none
Wiz (Motion picture)	PN1997.W5873
Wizard of Oz (Motion picture)	PN1997.W593
Wolf man (Motion picture)	none
Zardoz (Motion picture)	none

VI
TELEVISION AND RADIO PROGRAM MAIN ENTRIES AND CLASSIFICATION NUMBERS

INTRODUCTION

Books about specific television programs are classed in PN1992.77, radio programs in PN1991.77. Each program receives a unique subject cutter derived from the first letter of the show's title; a second cutter for main entry completes the classification for particular books. The subject heading for each show is its name plus the appellation (Television program) or (Radio program).

Alfred Hitchcock presents (Television program)	PN1992.77.A479
Amazing stories (Television program)	none
Avengers (Television program)	PN1992.77.A923
Batman (Television program)	PN1992.77.B343
Battlestar Galactica (Television program)	PN1992.77.B353
Dark shadows (Television program)	PN1992.77.D343
Day after (Television program)	none
Doctor Who (Television program)	PN1992.77.D6273
Fireball XL5 (Television program)	PN1992.77.F53
Flash Gordon (Television program)	none
Get Smart (Television program)	PN1992.77.G4773
Girl from U.N.C.L.E. (Television program)	PN1992.77.G553
Incredible Hulk (Television program)	none
Jonny Quest (Television program)	PN1992.77.J663
Land of the giants (Television program)	none
Logan's run (Television program)	none
Lost in space (Television program)	PN1992.77.L673
Man from U.N.C.L.E. (Television program)	PN1992.77.M2653
Martian chronicles (Television program)	none
Mork & Mindy (Television program)	PN1992.77.M66
Muppet show (Television program)	PN1992.77.M853
Night gallery (Television program)	none
Outer limits (Television program)	PN1992.77.O983
Planet of the apes (Television program)	none
Prisoner (Television program)	PN1992.77.P7

Return of the man from U.N.C.L.E. (Television program)	PN1992.77.R483
Robotech (Television program)	PN1992.77.R543
Science fiction theater (Television program)	none
Space 1999 (Television program)	none
Spider-Man (Television program)	PN1992.77.S643
Star trek (Television program)	PN1992.77.S73
Star trek—the animated series (Television program)	PN1992.77.S734
Star trek—the next generation (Television program)	none
Starlost (Television program)	none
Starman (Television program)	none
Stingray (Television program)	PN1992.77.S753
Superman (Television program)	PN1992.77.S83
Tales of tomorrow (Television program)	none
Time tunnel (Television program)	none
Tom Corbett, space cadet (Television program)	none
Twilight zone (Television program)	PN1992.77.T87
V (Television program)	PN1992.77.V183
Voyage to the bottom of the sea (Television program)	none
World War III (Television program)	none

RADIO PROGRAMS

Hitchhiker's guide to the galaxy (Radio program)	none
War of the worlds (Radio program)	none

VII
COMIC STRIP MAIN ENTRIES AND CLASSIFICATION NUMBERS

INTRODUCTION

Comic books, strips, etc., are classified into PN6728, cuttered by the first letter of the title, and cuttered again by main entry of the book. The subject heading is the name of the comic plus the appellation (Comic strip). As this is a fairly new development, relatively few comics have received numbers thus far.

Avengers (Comic strip)	PN6728.A9
Barbarella (Comic strip)	none
Batman (Comic strip)	PN6728.B36
Captain America (Comic strip)	PN6728.C35
Doctor Strange (Comic strip)	PN6728.D58
Fantastic four (Comic strip)	PN6728.F33
Howard the duck (Comic strip)	PN6728.H68
Hulk (Comic strip)	PN6728.H8
Spider-Man (Comic strip)	PN6728.S6
Superman (Comic strip)	PN6728.S9
X-Men (Comic strip)	PN6728.X2

ABOUT THE AUTHOR

Michael Burgess is Chief Cataloger (with the rank of full Professor) at California State University, San Bernardino, having previously served there as Periodicals Librarian, reference librarian, and Assistant Head of Acquisitions. His first book was published in May of 1970, four months before he joined the CSUSB faculty; in the eighteen years since that auspicious debut, he has authored over a hundred articles and reviews, edited a dozen scholarly series for Arno Press, Newcastle Publishing Co., Starmont House, and Borgo Press, and written or edited two score volumes for Gale Research Co., Arno Press, Times Books, Newcastle, ABC-Clio, Libraries Unlimited, and Starmont House, among others. On Oct. 11, 1983, he entered the 10,000,000th bibliographical record into the OCLC cataloging database. A member of the California Faculty Association, he was appointed to the state-wide Librarians' Task Force in 1986, and edits their *LTF Newsletter*. In 1987, his many achievements were honored by his campus when he was given a $2500 Meritorious Performance and Professional Promise award. This, the publication of his fortieth book, happily coincides with the celebration of his fortieth birthday.

www.ingramcontent.com/pod-product-compliance
Lightning Source LLC
LaVergne TN
LVHW041623070426
835507LV00008B/426